The development of *Jubilee Celebrations 3* was made possible through a grant from Schowalter Foundation, Inc., Newton, Kansas.

This publication uses the New Revised Standard Version of the Bible, copyright © 1989, by the Division of Christian Education of the National Council of Churches of Christ in the U.S.A. Used by permission.

Cover design by Merrill Miller

00 99 98 97 96 5 4 3 2 1

Library of Congress Cataloging-in-Publication Data

Harnish, Dorothy M., 1941-
    Jubilee celebrations.
    p.   cm.

    Includes bibliographical references.
    1. Worship programs. I. Title.
BV198.H37 1994   93-43573
ISBN 0-87178-477-7 (pbk. :v.1)
ISBN 0-87178-475-0 (pbk. :v. 2)
ISBN 0-87178-476-9 (pbk. :v.3)

Printed in the United States of America

Contents

The Spirit of the Lord is upon me,
because he has anointed me
to bring good news to the poor.
He has sent me to proclaim release to the captives
and recovery of sight to the blind,
to let the oppressed go free,
to proclaim the year of the Lord's favor.

—Luke 4:18-19

Preface

Whosoever walks towards God one cubit, God runs towards him twain.
—Jewish Proverb

We believe that the Holy Spirit has been at work in the midst of creating these celebrations. The Holy Spirit has breathed a freshness into these pages. We trust that as you gather together to plan a celebration or reenact a festival, the Holy Spirit will continue to move. Listen for the Holy Spirit in your planning as you create, work, struggle, and grow together. Look for the Holy Spirit in your congregation where you will find hidden talent and many who are willing and eager to work on celebrative events. Receive the Holy Spirit in your church as you expand the traditional patterns of worship and learning to new shapes and squiggles.

The Holy Spirit will inspire you in creating a holy, spiritual, unique, fresh experience of nurture and worship especially for your congregation.

—Brenda Glanzer and Mariann Martin

Introduction

How to use this book

These celebrations are for the whole church and require cooperation between pastors, worship committees, and education committees. The first item of business is to set up a meeting of key people from each group to plan a celebration. Then use the following list as an agenda.

1. Pick a date for your celebration and begin planning at least eight weeks ahead.

2. Plan for a 1½ - to 2-hour time period to celebrate. Dispense with the regular worship time and Sunday school time. The celebration will accomplish both. Allow 30-45 minutes in each celebration for activities.

3. Modify. These celebrations were written for the typical church with a sanctuary, fellowship hall, and classrooms, an active Sunday school, and a multi-talented membership. If this doesn't describe your congregation, modify the plan to fit your people and facilities.

4. Activities are designed for school-age children through adults. Provide your usual care for preschoolers, infants, and toddlers.

5. Permission is granted, *unless otherwise indicated,* to reproduce prayers, litanies, and music in worship bulletins, provided that no part of such reproduction is sold or distributed beyond the event held in the local church and provided that proper credit is given to the original author.

6. If suggested hymns are unfamiliar, replace them with hymns from your congregation's hymnal or songbooks.

7. Invite guest speakers early to avoid schedule conflicts, and allow them plenty of time to prepare.

8. Assign leaders, musicians, and teachers in advance. They will need time to gather supplies, rehearse, and prepare presentations. Materials for activities are too numerous to include in the "You will need" section. Urge activity leaders to read their instructions early and gather all necessary items, remembering that in many cases participants will come to the activity centers in shifts.

9. To help you prepare, a sample bulletin is provided in each celebration. You may wish to include information that is specific to your event, such as hymn choices and locations of activity centers.

10. Brief instructions for activities are included in each celebration. Leaders may need to expand activities or try them out ahead of time to ensure smooth sailing on the day of the celebration. In very large congregations, duplicate activity centers to accommodate more people in small groups. Be prepared to direct people to the location of each activity center.

11. Several celebrations suggest a topic for a sermon or homily. The pastor may use the suggested topic or create a new one. Or the planning committee may decide to use an alternative to the sermon, such as a videotape or drama.

12. Promote the celebration four weeks ahead of time on posters and in church newsletters, bulletins, the newspaper religion section, and Sunday school handouts.

13. Many of the resources suggested in ***Jubilee Celebrations 3*** are found in *Hymnal: A Worship Book*. The hymnal can be ordered from either Brethren Press (1451 Dundee Avenue, Elgin, IL 60120-1694, 800-771-3712), Faith & Life Press (Box 347, Newton, KS 67114-0347, 800-743-2484), or Mennonite Publishing House (616 Walnut Avenue, Scottdale, PA 15683-1999, 800-245-7894).

The options for use of *Jubilee* celebrations are unlimited. Some congregations will find that Sunday evening worship, retreats, midweek services, or holiday programs are more appropriate times for *Jubilee* celebrations. Planning committees may wish to use portions of these celebrations for other occasions, and variation is possible and encouraged. Whatever form a celebration takes, it should uphold the philosophy of ***Jubilee Celebrations***, whose intent is to unify children and adults, worship and nurture.

About the authors

Brenda Glanzer is an ordained minister in the General Conference Mennonite Church and serves as a chaplain at the Via Christi Health Care System, St. Joseph campus, in Wichita, Kansas. One of her enduring passions is to bring the Bible to life.

Mariann Martin, a native of Mercersburg, Pennsylvania, teaches theater and speech at Hesston College in Hesston, Kansas. One of her loves is drama in worship.

Side-by-Side
Celebrating a New Church School Year

While we teach, we learn.

—Seneca

The beginning of a new church school year is the time to renew our vow to be open to the leading of the Holy Spirit, to say, "I want to learn whatever you have to teach me." It is also the time to commit ourselves to being the instruments through which others learn what the Holy Spirit is saying. In the church everyone is a learner and a teacher. We have a lot to share and a lot to learn. No one has the lessons of life and spirituality completely figured out. No one can sit idly by and expect to continue learning. We must walk side-by-side, look, and listen for the signs God sends to guide us on the road. We must encourage each other to be active learners and teachers for a lifetime.

Bible Text

Luke 24:13-32

Bible Background for Our Celebration

On the third day after the crucifixion, two of Jesus' disciples were walking from Jerusalem to Emmaus. As they walked they discussed the events of the past week. They talked about the painful death of their friend Jesus. They shared their dashed hopes that he would be the one to redeem Israel. They wondered about the mysterious disappearance of his body from the tomb. A stranger joined them and asked what they were talking about. They couldn't believe someone had not heard of Jesus of Nazareth. They proceeded to tell of his power and his unfair death sentence. Little did they know they were actually walking with the resurrected Jesus!

Jesus had given the disciples the information they needed to be able to understand the events of his death and his return to life on earth. In the very real distress of those times, however, the teachings of Jesus were cloudy, confusing, and at times seemingly irrelevant to the disciples. In resurrected form, as in life, Jesus was the teacher. He began by asking questions and listening to their hurt and confusion. He began where they were, both emotionally and intellectually.

When the disciples spoke of doubt and confusion, Jesus did what many teachers feel like doing at one time or another: He said with exasperation, "How slow you are!" But then Jesus helped them along, unfolding the story of faith more fully for their understanding, beginning with Moses and the prophets.

At their encouragement, Jesus stayed to eat with them. Then he broke bread with them, one of the rituals he had taught them to do. Suddenly they recognized him and their eyes were opened. Only when the faith story and their personal experience connected, did they understand. This is what Christian educator Thomas Groome calls the "aha!" moment. Jesus knew they needed that "aha" experience to be able to continue the ministry and teaching he had started. Those are the same moments we all crave as we grow in faith and stature. May we follow Christ's example of listening, teaching, and modeling as we interact with one another. Let us be teachers to one another, listening, questioning, and challenging one another in our daily walk together.

Faith Nugget

The moments of sudden understanding in Christian faith happen in the side-by-side journey with Jesus and other Christian travelers.

Early Preparation

Select actors for the opening drama and provide them scripts at least four weeks before the celebration. This will allow them time to coordinate rehearsals and memorize lines. Ask a third person to attend rehearsals to act as director and give the actors feedback from the audience's perspective. At least four rehearsals are recommended to ensure naturalness and ease.

The musicians who play instruments for the hymns should also be notified a month in advance. They need ample time to coordinate rehearsals and gather unique rhythm instruments. Likewise, the storyteller will need a copy of the interactive Emmaus road story to rehearse and memorize so that it flows smoothly. Assign the construction of road signs and banner to the youth group or others.

There is a time in the celebration for four speakers to share from personal experience. Invite the speakers early so they can reflect and prepare. Give them a time limit and encourage them to sketch out remarks on paper to stay within the allotted time. Be sure to have an extra person in mind in case you need a replacement.

In the month or weeks before the celebration, announce that a special book offering will be taken during the celebration. In addition to their monetary offerings, ask people to bring an offering of used books in good condition or new books for the church library. Ask for books that are inspirational for the Christian journey or helpful in understanding the Bible.

You will need

- ❏ road signs
- ❏ a banner
- ❏ Sunday school study materials and a basket of bread for the worship center table
- ❏ six speakers for two-minute reflections
- ❏ a storyteller
- ❏ musicians to play guitar and rhythm instruments
- ❏ a police costume
- ❏ craft supplies and paper for each group to create a symbol and a blessing
- ❏ Sunday school teachers to guide the process in blessing delivery

Name of your church
Side-by-Side
Celebrating a New Church School Year

Meal

Gathering Hymn ...."Here in this place"

Drama ...."Keep Moving"

Hymn................."Jesus, we want to meet"

Litany

Prayer

Children's Story......................"No Parking"

Hymns........................"Teach me, O Lord"
"O little children, gather"

Reflections of Learners and Teachers
[list names here]

Blessings Groups

Gather Again

Hymn..........................."Bwana awabariki"

Exchange of Blessings for Learning and Teaching

Prayer

Offerings of Books and Money

Hymn........................."Move in our midst"

Sending

The Celebration

Throughout the area where you will hold the celebration, post street signs that say NO PARKING, ONE WAY, NO LOITERING, NO STOPPING, CONSTRUCTION AHEAD, YIELD, or MERGE. At the entrance to the area, place a sign that says PLEASE ENTER. Have it resemble the familiar DO NOT ENTER sign and attach it to a microphone stand, placed where it can be seen. At the place where the drama will be staged, hang a banner with figures of two people walking side-by-side. Add lettering to the banner proclaiming CELEBRATING A NEW SUNDAY SCHOOL YEAR.

On a table at the center of the celebration space, display an open Bible, a Bible commentary, copies of Sunday school materials, storybooks, story figures, and a SCHOOL ZONE sign. Arrange these items around a large basket of bread (slices or rolls).

Gathering

This celebration emphasizes that we continue to learn our whole lives and we are teachers to each other in our daily routines. Begin the time together with an ordinary meal such as donuts and juice for breakfast or sandwiches and soup for lunch or dinner.

Gathering Hymn

Come together during an instrumental rendition of "Here in this place" or other gathering hymn. When everyone is present, sing the hymn together.

Drama: "Keep Moving"

Present the drama "Keep Moving," found in Resources for This Celebration. The congregational hymn is interrupted by the blowing of a whistle and the shouts of a uniformed officer entering carrying a stop sign. The uniform should be clearly bogus so as not to frighten anyone. A big silver star of aluminum foil would do the trick. For a more elaborate touch, try to get a keystone cop costume.

Hymn

Sing "Jesus, we want to meet" or another song about Jesus the teacher. "Jesus, we want to meet" works well with the accompaniment of a hand drum and rhythm instruments.

Litany

Leader: This day we celebrate and bless a new school year.

Teachers: A year of teaching.

Students: A year of learning.

Teachers: A year for questions of doubt or challenge.

Students: A year for statements of faith and affirmation.

Teachers: A year to hear from each other.

Students: A year to read from God's word.

Teachers: A year of active listening.

Students: A year of active seeking.

Teachers: A year of learning.

Students: A year of teaching.

Prayer

Teach us, O Lord, to walk in your steps, to listen to your voice, to share our burdens with one another. Oh, great Teacher, teach us to learn.

Help us, O Lord, to walk with each other, to listen with your ears, to carry the burdens of one another. Oh, great Teacher, help us to teach. Amen.

Children's Story: "No Parking"

Gather the children and talk about the beginning of the school year. Informally ask the following questions, pausing between each question for responses:

• What do you think was the most important thing you learned in all your years of school so far?

- What was the hardest lesson you had?
- Is there a subject in school that you don't understand very well?
- What do you think makes a good teacher?

Then say, "Jesus was a great teacher. He taught his disciples lessons about God and how to live life by telling stories and riddles and object lessons. He gave them assignments and expected reports. He gave pop quizzes now and then. He asked questions and listened to his students' answers. He even had snack time in the middle of lessons and took them on field trips. Even so, the disciples didn't always find it easy to understand what they were supposed to learn. This is the story of the disciples finally catching on to the biggest lesson of all."

Conclude this time by telling the story called "No Parking" found in the resource section of this celebration. Involve the children as you tell the story. Divide them into groups of three. Explain that in each group, two will be learners (disciples) and one will be the teacher (Jesus). Give them a moment to choose roles. Instruct teachers to put their hands over their faces and sit down quickly when you give them a cue to "disappear." Rehearse this action. Then ask learners to stand and act out all the actions of the story by following your lead as you pantomime the capitalized words.

Hymn

Sing hymns such as "Teach me, O Lord" (in Resources for This Celebration) or "O little children, gather."

Reflections of Learners and Teachers

A host moderates as three people (children, youth, and adults) share two-minute reflections or tributes to favorite Sunday school teachers past or present. The host then invites three teachers (Sunday school teachers or school teachers) in the congregation to present two-minute reflections about a lesson they learned from a particular student or from a teaching experience in general. Suggest that these speeches be inspirational in nature. Many

people find it difficult to stick to time limits. Emphasize the limit very clearly but also plan some cushion time around this part of the service. The host may close with a brief summary of the ideas in the introduction and Bible background for this celebration. (Note: If your church has a mentoring program, this would be a good time to recognize the mentoring pairs by having mentors present a Bible or devotional book to their partners.)

Blessings for Learners and Teachers

Help the congregation organize themselves into groups made up of people born in the same month. Prepare a station for every month of the year (or every two or three months of the year if you are a small group). Each group will create a symbol and a blessing for learning or teaching to be delivered to another group when the whole group gathers again. Decide beforehand who will bless whom.

Equip each group with craft supplies to make the assigned symbol.

January—clay for making small oil lamps to symbolize enlightenment

February—permanent markers or tempera paint for decorating light bulbs representing bright ideas

March—construction paper and odds and ends to make hearts symbolizing compassion

April—colorful pictures from old magazines to make paper chains symbolizing the links to better understanding

May—cardboard and foil to make keys representing the key to unlocking the truth

June—paper and cardboard to replicate a sun dial symbolizing the patience to wait upon God to speak

July—paper to make megaphones to increase our ability to learn by hearing

August—plastic magnifying sheets cut into interesting shapes to increase our ability to learn by seeing

September—foil to sculpt miniature barbells symbolizing the strength to keep learning

October—yarn or paper to make friendship bands representing the way we learn from each other

November—odds and ends to decorate

gloves unclaimed from lost and found, symbolizing our ability to reach others with the good news

December—modeling clay to make empty vessels symbolizing a willingness to remain open to new learnings of faith

Have each group write a blessing to read to another group when the symbols are exchanged. Suggest that they choose verses 26, 33, 66, or 103 in Psalm 119 or Matthew 5:6.

Gather Again

A musical interlude is the signal to clean up stations and return to the full group.

Hymn

As people are moving back to the celebration area, sing a chorus such as "Bwana awabariki" as many times as needed to draw everyone back together (see Resources for This Celebration). Accompany "Bwana awabariki" with drums and rhythm instruments.

Blessings Exchange

A leader calls two groups at a time to the center of the celebration to exchange blessings and symbols. Leave the symbols at the worship center.

Prayer

The leader closes the blessing exchange with this short prayer:

Dear Lord, thank you for modeling for us the role of a listening, creative teacher. Thank you for investing time and energy in the growth of your students. We thank you that we are all your students. Bless our new Sunday school year as we seek to know you better. Walk with us as you walked with your disciples. Keep us moving and help us to enter the active process of learning. May we see you as you move in our midst. Amen.

Offering

Receive the usual offering of monetary gifts, but also invite people to bring books for the church library to the celebration worship as a way to support education in the church. As people are bringing books and offerings to the worship center sing the chorus of a hymn such as "Guide my feet."

Hymn

Sing "Move in our midst" (see Resources for This Celebration).

Sending

The cop from the opening skit re-enters during the hymn, blowing his whistle as one of the rhythm instruments. He dismisses everyone by saying "Let's be moving along now" and giving a final blow of his whistle.

Resources for This Celebration

Keep Moving

Cop: Whoa! Hey! Stop the music! [*whistle*]

Songster: What's going on?

Cop: Sorry, I'm closing you down.

Songster: Why?

Cop: The Chief said so.

Songster: Who?

Cop: The Chief of the Local Ways and Means Committee has declared that henceforward there shall be no Sunday school taking place here.

Songster: What? I've never heard of the Chief of the Ways and Means Committee. How can he do that?

Cop: He has ways. And he means it, too.

Songster: Why? What are we doing wrong?

Cop: I'm takin' ya in on a loitering charge. There is too much sitting around, doing nothing, happening here. We got places for people who do that. Ever heard of "Sing Sing"?

Songster: Wait a minute! We're not doing nothing. We're singing!

Cop: Disturbing the peace is what you mean. Can't you see that guy trying to sleep back there?

Songster: We read scripture here, too.

Cop: Heard all about it. Chief's issued a warrant for that, too.

Songster: What?

Cop: Speeding.

Songster: We may read it fast, but we take our time in class discussions. Doesn't that make up for it?

Cop: Those class discussions are on my list, too. Digging through other people's trash is against the law. [*Person in congregation gets up and exits as if going to use the facilities, or a person in the congregation arrives late and walks in looking for a place to sit.*] See that? Got a warrant for that, too.

Songster: That, too?

Cop: Jaywalking. Look, the Chief says this building is a one-way, no parking zone, and you're violating the law. Gonna have to fine ya and take ya all in. [*whips out ticket book*]

Songster: Now wait, don't make us leave, we just got settled in. Would you let us stay if we pay the fine? How much will it be? We could take up a collection.

Cop: Let's see. Sitting idly with the engines off in a no parking zone—$50. Sliding backwards in a one-way zone—$50. Disturbing the peace, jaywalking, loitering, dumpster-digging, and speeding. That's $50 each—adds up to $350.

Songster: Three hundred dollars? We can come up with that if we need to. Treasurer, will you get the offering plates?

Cop: [*tears off ticket*]There ya go.

Songster: Hey, this says $700! I thought you said $350.

Cop: Had to fine ya double. You're in a school zone.

Songster: Come on. Can't you go easy on us? We didn't know.

Cop: Ignorance of the law is no excuse.

Songster: Please officer? We'll try to do better.

Cop: Operating a Sunday school is a privilege, ya know, not a right. Chief can take it away from you if you're not going to use it properly, ya know.

Songster: We know, officer.

Cop: Privileges come with responsibility, ya know.

Songster: Yes, we know, officer.

Cop: I got every reason to haul you in, ya know.

Songster: Yes, we know, officer.

Cop: Well, now. Tell ya what I'm going to do. You look like a nice bunch of folks. I won't bring ya in front of the judge this time, okay? I'll just let you off this time with a verbal warning.

Songster: Thank you, officer.

Cop: Be careful in that school zone, you hear? Have a nice morning. Keep moving now. [*Everyone exits as the cop repeats the instruction "Keep moving."*]

No Parking

The two disciples were WALKING [*in place*] down the road to a town called Emmaus. One WIPED HER EYES. The other WIPED HIS EYES AND BLEW HIS NOSE. They both SHOOK THEIR HEADS SLOWLY. They WALKED farther. The one STOMPED HIS FOOT. The other SHRUGGED HER SHOULDERS. They both SIGHED. They each WIPED THEIR EYES. You see, they were Jesus' disciples and he had just been killed. They couldn't understand it. They SCRATCHED THEIR HEADS and tried to remember all that Jesus had taught them. They LIFTED THEIR HEADS to think of all the wonderful things he had said about his kingdom in the future. They LOWERED THEIR HEADS when they thought about how he died. They SIGHED "How can this be?"

Suddenly a third person was WALKING with them. It was Jesus but they didn't recognize him. He LOOKED AT HIS DISCIPLES, his students he had tried to prepare for this day. He ASKED THEM WHAT WAS WRONG? They TOLD HIM HOW JESUS HAD DIED ON A CROSS. Jesus SHOOK HIS HEAD SADLY. He TILTED HIS HEAD to listen to them explain more about how sad and confused they were. They continued to WALK side-by-side. Jesus NODDED HIS HEAD as he listened. He TOUCHED THEIR ARMS to comfort them. The disciples SCRATCHED THEIR HEADS AND SPREAD OUT THEIR HANDS as they told of the story about the women seeing the empty tomb that morning.

Then Jesus PUT UP A HAND and began to speak. He SIGHED because his students still didn't understand. He PUT UP HIS FIRST FINGER as if to tell them one thing that the prophets had written about him. He PUT UP A SECOND FINGER as he reminded them of another. He PUT UP EACH FINGER as he reminded his students of all the lessons he had taught them from the scripture that prophesied about his death.

They WALKED A LITTLE BIT FASTER. They were becoming excited by what this man was saying. They PUT THEIR HANDS OVER THEIR HEARTS because their hearts felt warm and were beating fast.

Then they STOPPED WALKING for they were at their house. They invited Jesus to come in with them. They SAT DOWN TO EAT. Jesus TOOK A PIECE OF BREAD [*from the basket on the table*]. He LIFTED IT UP and blessed it. Then he BROKE IT AND HANDED IT TO THE

DISCIPLES. They OPENED THEIR EYES WIDE. Then he DISAPPEARED.

The disciples SMILED. They JUMPED for joy! They finally figured out that the man who had been walking with them explaining scripture was their very own teacher, Jesus. They SHOUTED, "He is risen!" They RAN all the way back to Jerusalem to tell the others. Jesus' followers became the leaders, telling everyone about Jesus. Now you are the leaders. When you leave this place, go and tell everyone what you know about Jesus!

Teach me, O Lord

BISHOP LM

1 Teach me, O Lord, thy way of truth, and from it
2 In thy com-mand-ments make me walk, for in thy
3 Turn thou my eyes from van - i - ty, and cause me
4 Turn thou a - way re-proach and fear. Thy right-eous

I will not de-part; that I may stead - fast -
law my joy shall be. Give me a heart that
in thy ways to tread. O let thy ser - vant
judg - ments I con - fess. To know thy pre - cepts

ly o - bey, give me an un - der - stand - ing heart.
loves thy will, from dis - con - tent and en - vy free.
prove thy word, and thus to god - ly fear be led.
I de - sire. Re - vive me in thy right - eous - ness.

Text: based on Psalm 119:33-40, *Psalter*, 1912
Music: Joseph P. Holbrook, *The Presbyterian Hymnal*, 1874

Bwana awabariki
(May God grant you a blessing)

BISHOP LM

1 Bwa - na a - wa - ba - ri - ki, Bwa - na a - wa - ba - ri - ki,
2 May God grant you a bless - ing, may God grant you a bless - ing,

Bwa - na a - wa - ba - ri - ki mi - le - le.
may God grant you a bless - ing ev - er - more.

U - ki - mcha Bwa - na. Bwa - na a - wa - ba - ri - ki.
Re - vere the Lord. May God grant you a bless - ing.

Text: Swahili folk hymn
Music: Swahili melody

Move in our midst

PINE GLEN 99. 99

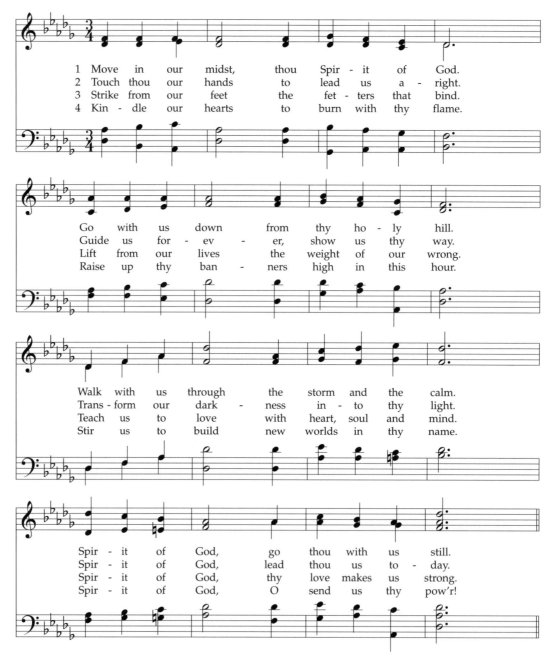

1 Move in our midst, thou Spir - it of God.
2 Touch thou our hands to lead us a - right.
3 Strike from our feet the fet - ters that bind.
4 Kin - dle our hearts to burn with thy flame.

Go with us down from thy ho - ly hill.
Guide us for - ev - er, show us thy way.
Lift from our lives the weight of our wrong.
Raise up thy ban - ners high in this hour.

Walk with us through the storm and the calm.
Trans - form our dark - ness in - to thy light.
Teach us to love with heart, soul and mind.
Stir us to build new worlds in thy name.

Spir - it of God, go thou with us still.
Spir - it of God, lead thou us to - day.
Spir - it of God, thy love makes us strong.
Spir - it of God, O send us thy pow'r!

Text: Kenneth I. Morse, 1942, 1949, *The Brethren Hymnal*, 1951
Music: Perry L. Huffaker, 1950, *The Brethren Hymnal*, 1951

The Festival of Booths
Celebrating Thanksgiving

He who is full of joy is full of love for human beings and all fellow creatures.
—Ba'al Shem Tov

When the English pilgrims came to North America and survived their first year in the new land, they celebrated with a three-day feast. Some historians believe that the feast was modeled after the Old Testament festival of *Sukkot*, also called the Feast of Tabernacles or the Festival of Booths. *Sukkot* is a celebration that does double duty. It rejoices in the harvest and teaches the valuable lessons of faith history. It exalts in God's care, provision, and plan for his people.

During this eight-day festival, the Jews were commanded to build huts or booths called *sukkahs*. These booths were like the temporary shelters made from branches by the Hebrews in the wilderness and like the huts made by the vinedressers when they lived in the vineyard during the harvest, guarding the crop and working long hours. Later on, festival observers were to eat and sleep in rustic booths for one week. Celebrating this festival is important to Christians who also celebrate God's provision for his people. Our enactment of the festival will not be exact. There are many rules governing the rituals, prayers, and the building of booths. We will attempt some of these practices, but rather than hold to the letter of the law, our primary aim is to be thankful and joyous for God's provision for us, even in the "wilderness."

Bible Text

Leviticus 23:33-44; Deuteronomy 16:13-15; Nehemiah 8:9-18; John 7.

Bible Background for Our Festival

The children of Israel fled Egypt under God's protection and wandered in the desert for forty years. All the time they roamed, they lived in *sukkahs,* or temporary shelters. In Leviticus God gives Moses instructions to relay to the people before they enter the promised land and are scattered. In Leviticus 23, one of the *mitzvah* (commandments) states that the people should build booths and live in them for a week so their "generations may know that I made the people of Israel live in booths when I brought them out of the land of Egypt: I am the Lord your God."

The festival was scheduled to be held after the grain harvests. It was the perfect time for a festival of thanksgiving and merriment to remind a settled farming people that they were once wanderers under God's care.

Centuries after settling in the promised land, the Israelites disobeyed God, forgot the Torah, and became slaves again, this time to the Babylonians. Nehemiah 8 tells how the Jews were liberated once again, reclaimed their faith, rebuilt the walls of Jerusalem, and read the Torah together. Ezra, the priest, brought out the Book of the Law of Moses and began to read it to the people gathered at the newly constructed Water Gate. The people wept when they heard how many of the laws they had forgotten.

As they were reviving their faith, they realized the time was near for the beginning of *Sukkot* (the Festival of Booths), a celebration of joy. So the people were instructed, "This day is holy to the Lord your God; Do not mourn or weep" (Neh. 8:9). They were told to enjoy choice foods and sweet drinks and to send some to those who have nothing prepared. Again they were told, "Do not be grieved, for the joy of the Lord is your strength" (Neh. 8:10). The next day they

continued to read the rules for booth-building and followed them. The renewed festival was apparently quite a celebration and Nehemiah states that their joy was very great.

The Festival of Booths was celebrated regularly in Jesus' lifetime as recorded in John 7. The eighth day of *Sukkot* culminates in a joyous, noisy, sustained prayer for rain to ensure well-watered crops the following year. Celebrants ask for the renewing winter rains that will change the now dry, brown earth back into a realm of green. It was on this last and greatest day of the feast that Jesus stood and said in a loud voice, "Let anyone who is thirsty come to me and let the one who believes in me drink. As the scripture has said, 'Out of the believer's heart shall flow rivers of living water' " (vv. 37-38).

Throughout the Bible, the Festival of the Booths is heralded as a main event of the year. It is truly a time of great celebration.

Early Preparation

Faith Nugget

We thank God for faithful leading, streams of renewal, and provision for our needs.

The two festivals in this book are approximate reenactments of actual biblical festivals. For this festival, *Sukkot*, assign several handy people to build an actual-size booth of lumber or branches that will be used as the focal point for the festival. (See the illustration on the first page of this festival.) As part of the festival, people will adorn the booth with traditional decorations.

Choose someone who can learn the dance described in the festival and teach it to the congregation.

You will need

- ❏ leaders for the activity centers
- ❏ boxed or canned foods and baskets
- ❏ lumber and nails or screws for the booth
- ❏ leafy branches and decorations for the booth
- ❏ branches of palm (pine branches or corn husks may be used if palm is unavailable)
- ❏ branches of willow
- ❏ branches of myrtle or another leafy tree
- ❏ *etrog* (lemons may be used)
- ❏ eight readers
- ❏ shoe boxes, scissors, and decorations for the miniature *sukkahs*

Name of your church

The Festival of Booths

Celebrating Thanksgiving

Gathering Hymns.........."What is this place"
"For the fruit of all creation"
"We give thanks unto you"

Learning About Sukkot

Time with the Children ...."The Lulv and
the Etrog"

Sukkot Centers

1. Decorate the Sukkah
2. Make Miniature Sukkahs
3. Make the Lulav
4. A Thanksgiving Meditation
5. Learn a Traditional Dance
6. Read the Faith Story
7. Share the Abundant Harvest

Gather Again for the Festival

Gathering Music

Dance of Thanksgiving

Words of Welcome

Reading of the Faith History

Offering ...."What gift can we bring"

Rain and Water Celebration.............."Psalm
Collage"

Hymn..."Hosanna, loud hosanna" (vv. 1,3)

Prayer

Preparation for the Festival

The first half of the festival will be spent learning about *Sukkot* and making preparations for the actual festival observance. The second half is reserved for reenacting some of the traditions of *Sukkot* as a way of celebrating our own Thanksgiving holiday.

Ahead of time, place the unadorned booth in the place where the festival will be held. Create a *lulav* (see Time with the Children). Place it in front of the booth.

Gathering Hymns

Sing several gathering hymns such as "What is this place," "For the fruit of all creation," or "We give thanks unto you." This last hymn has a Jewish folk song rhythm. If you use this hymn, a simple dance step could be added. And a soloist could lead the call and response that is built into the hymn.

Learning about *Sukkot*

A leader shares this information with the congregation:

Since Christianity has grown out of the Jewish tradition, we claim the practices of the Hebrew people as the foundation of our own traditions in the Christian faith. The Hebrew practices are, after all, the traditions Jesus may have practiced. The Jewish year is marked by festivals much as ours is marked by Christmas, Easter, and Pentecost. One such Jewish festival is the Festival of Booths or *Sukkot*, an ancient harvest custom that predates our own Thanksgiving by thousands of years.

When the Pilgrims survived their first year in a new land and gathered their first harvests, they celebrated with a feast. Historians believe that since the Pilgrims knew the Bible well, they may have modeled their feast after the Feast of Tabernacles, another name for the Festival of Booths. They too were a wan-dering people in a new land and were thankful for God's provision. The instructions to celebrate the Festival of Booths were given to Moses in Leviticus. The children of Israel had not yet settled in the promised land, but God knew they would soon be farmers with harvests and that they would soon be settled. They needed a reminder that they were once wanderers, freed from slavery by God who cared for them.

During this festival, God commanded a group campout of sorts. The people were to construct a booth like we see in front of us today and live in it for a week. God states in Leviticus the reason for such a custom: "So that your generations will know that I made the people of Israel live in booths when I brought them out of the land of Egypt: I am the Lord your God." Listen to the instructions as they are stated in Leviticus. [*Reader reads Leviticus 23:33-44.*] Deuteronomy also records the importance of celebrating the Feast of the Tabernacles, another name for the celebration. [*Reader reads Deuteronomy 16:13-15.*]

Jewish books elaborating on the festival explain the practice of booth-building in more detail. The booth, or *sukkah*, must be temporary. It is to represent the dwellings that the Jews used while wandering in the desert. It is a reminder of the Jewish exodus, a living history lesson—and a reminder of God's care during the time of uprootedness. It is also said that building booths was typical at harvest time. The fields were far from the houses. The farmers wanted to gather ripe crops as quickly as possible, so they worked from sunup to sundown, sleeping overnight in the temporary shacks built in the fields.

Since the festival is also designed to pass along faith heritage, children must help build the family booth. It provides an excellent opportunity for teaching moments. The *sukkah* may be built against a wall and have two, three, or four walls. The ceiling, however, must not be closed in completely. Leafy boughs are usually placed on a few support beams across the top. One must be able to see through the ceiling so that one can look at the stars at night. The lack of protection from the weather provides a reminder of how fragile and dependent on God we really are. It also reminds us of those who live in poverty and do not have shelter. Just as the roof of the booth is not closed off, so we must not close ourselves off to those in need. It is *mitzvah*, or a requirement, to eat and sleep in the *sukkah* at least twice during the week of the festival.

The mood during the Festival of Booths is one of celebration. It comes two weeks after the high holy days of Rosh Hashanah and Yom Kippur, which require difficult self-examination and repentance. *Sukkot* balances these serious days with thanksgiving and joy, a chance to start over. Sadness is forbidden on *Sukkot*. It is a special time set apart to remember that joy is holy. In Nehemiah, the Jews rediscovered the laws of Moses after a time of having forgotten them. They wept when they learned of the many ways they had disappointed God. However, they also discovered that they were reading the laws near the time specified for the Festival of Booths, *Sukkot*. The priest and the Levities hurried to calm the people and proclaim that on this sacred day no sorrow was allowed! They began to enact the festival as the law commanded, and the sadness turned to celebration. The Bible says their joy was very great. Listen to the scriptures tell of this time. [*Reader reads Nehemiah 8:1, 9-17.*]

It is commanded that the festival be celebrated with beauty. Even though the booth is fairly fragile, it is richly decorated with fruits, popcorn, cranberry strings, flowers, and posters of famous people from the Old Testament. These people are invited in prayer to join the meals in the *sukkah*. Imagine asking Abraham, Sarah, Isaac, Rebekah, Jacob, Rachel, Leah, Joseph, Moses, Miriam, Aaron, Hannah, David, and Esther to eat with you. An extra plate may be set for the honored guests, but usually the extra place is filled with a needy guest. It is

thought that the honored ancestors would reject an invitation to any booth in which the poor were not welcome.

The table in the booth is set much as we set our Thanksgiving tables with nice plates and glasses, candles, places for guests, and a centerpiece of fruit or other reminders of blessing.

Time with the Children

A storyteller invites children to come into the booth to hear about the *lulav* and the *etrog*. Ask him or her to summarize the following information for the children.

Part of the Jewish tradition of the Festival of Booths includes a ceremony using the *lulav*. *Lulav* is actually the word for a palm branch, but in the festival the *lulav* is three different types of branches bunched together to create something like a pennant. It is carried along with a special fruit called the *etrog* or *citron*, which looks like a lumpy lemon. Festival observers carry the *lulav* in their right hand and the *etrog* in the left as they parade around the synagogue following a leader who holds the *Torah* or the scriptures. While prayers of blessing are being read, the people shake the *lulav* in six directions showing that God is everywhere [*demonstrate*]. When the name of God is spoken, however, the *lulav* is held still because God is the unshakable center of the universe. Some say the *lulav* and the *etrog* represent the fruits of Israel. Many wise Jewish teachers have offered their understandings of the custom.

To make a *lulav*, wrap three types of branches together: the palm, the willow, and the myrtle or other leafy tree. [*Have pieces at hand to show the children.*] Since the palm branch is the largest, the whole bunch is called the *lulav* or palm branch. Read or memorize and recite the explanations of the *lulav* and the *etrog* in the box on page 18.

Sukkot Centers

Give directions for moving to the activity centers. Allow people to change centers two or three times in the time allotted. Encourage adults to invite children to an activity center with them to mix the generations as much as possible.

1. Decorate the Sukkah. The booth is traditionally decorated by hanging fruits on strings from the ceiling, placing flowers and candles and pictures of Abraham in the booth, and laying branches across the ceiling. Decorate the *sukkah* for this festival in front of the sanctuary with fruits of the harvest and reminders of things we have to be thankful for. String popcorn, cranberries, and orange peel to make garlands. Make pictures of Abraham, families, farms, and foods to decorate the sides of the booth. Use beautiful squash, pumpkins, and corn. Or use odds and ends of paper, fabric, scrap wood, or plastic foam to make other decorations.

2. Make Miniature Sukkahs. A replica of the *sukkah* can be made by cutting a basic frame from a shoebox and laying twigs for the ceiling. After each person has made a *sukkah*, provide items such as wrapped candy, artificial fruits, flowers, and scraps to decorate them. Send the miniature *sukkahs* home to be used as a centerpiece for Thanksgiving tables, reminding people of God's faithfulness.

3. Make the *Lulav*. Wrap together a palm branch, three sprigs of myrtle or other leafy branch, and two sprigs of willow. The branches may be real or artificial. Substitute other kinds of branches if none of the traditional ones are available. In Eastern Europe, for instance, pine is used instead of palm; corn husks are another suggested substitution. The palm is placed in the middle, the myrtle on the right side, and the willow on the left. They are bound together by strands of palm. Carry the *lulav* in the right and the fruit in the left. Practice shaking the branches in six directions while the scriptures are being read. The six directions include north, south, east, west, up high, and down low (bend over rather than point the *lulav* to the floor). Be sure not to shake the *lulav* when God's name is mentioned. If there is extra time, use the palm fronds to braid rings or bracelets for the children. They can take these reminders home with them.

4. Take Time for a Thanksgiving Meditation.
Appoint a leader ahead of time to lead participants in a discussion about giving thanks. Brainstorm ways to incorporate grateful expressions into everyday life. Have people name reasons for which they are thankful to God, and encourage them to spend time in prayer reflecting on these ideas.

5. Learn a Traditional Dance.
Participants learn a simple dance step to the song "We give thanks unto you" or another eight-measure song in four-four time, such as "Asithi: Amen." Form two concentric circles with the inside circle facing out and the outer circle facing in. The dancers in each circle hold hands. The step is the same for each circle, but the circles will move in opposite directions.

> Beat 1: Stomp with the right foot.
> Beats 2 and 3: With weight still on the left foot, slide the right foot to the right (Beat 2) and step on Beat 3.
> Beat 4: Cross left foot behind the right foot.
> Beat 5: Step right with the right foot.
> Beat 6: Cross left foot in front of the right foot.
> Beat 7: Step right with the right foot.
> Beat 8: Shift weight to left foot. Get ready to begin again with a right foot stomp.

Continue in this pattern through the song. During the dance, hold hands high. If the group is coordinated enough to sing while dancing, have the center circle sing the call and the outer circle sing the response on the hymn. Or a leader standing on a chair in the center of the inside circle sings the call and the whole group of dancers sings the response. Inform the group that they will demonstrate the dance in the festival reenactment.

6. Read the Faith Story.
Nehemiah 9:4-36 offers a choral reading that was presented at the end of the *Sukkot* festival in the days when Israelites were rebuilding the walls of Jerusalem. Verse 4 suggests that sixteen readers stood on stairs and called back and forth before beginning the recitation of the faith journey. In this case, eight readers will practice the reading based on Nehemiah 9:4-21 for the festival. Try practicing in the space where the festival will be reenacted to make sure readers are able to project their voices to people seated away from them. Encourage them to read as though they were calling across a great distance to other readers. See the resource section of this festival for the choral reading of Nehemiah 9:4-21.

7. Share the Abundant Harvest.
In the weeks before the festival, collect boxed or canned food. Participants of this group will pack food baskets to be delivered to church members, a local food pantry, or people in the community who would benefit from such a gift. Include a handwritten note with each basket.

Gather Again for the Festival

Gathering Music

Play recorded Jewish liturgical music or hymns of thanksgiving as the congregation gathers.

Dance of Thanksgiving

The dancers who rehearsed during the activity time present their dance. Invite the congregation to join in singing.

Words of Welcome

Leader: Welcome to our special day of celebrating the Festival of Booths. On the seventh day of *Sukkot*, a special ceremony called *Hoshana Rabbah*, "the Great Salvation," is celebrated. During the festival, processions are made seven times around the synagogue carrying the *lulav* while scriptures are read and prayers are recited. As people process they shout "Hosanna" or "God Save Us!" [*Have the children give a practice shout.*] During a special ceremony on the eighth day, prayers are given in memory of deceased relatives and friends as a reminder of how fragile life is. Other prayers, noisy and sustained, are given for rain. We are going to do some of these things in our special celebration today. Welcome again to these expressions of joy and thanks-giving for God's care through the ages, especially for God's gift of salvation through Jesus Christ.

Reading of the Faith History

Readers stand in a loose circle around the festival area to joyfully read Nehemiah 9:4-21. Instruct the congregation to stand when the readers say "stand up." On this cue, begin a tape of prerecorded Jewish liturgical music, or have musicians play the tune to "We give thanks unto you" for processional music. Encourage able-bod-ied adults to lift small children onto their shoulders. Everyone who is able then lifts a *lulav* and *etrog* and begins to process around the sanctuary. The parade contin-ues around the sanctuary seven times. Reduce the volume of the music and have preassigned readers recite or read Psalms 113, 114, 117, 118 (you may cut verses 8-18 from this psalm if it is too long) into a microphone as others process. *Lulavs* are shaken while walking. Whenever the psalm calls "Praise the Lord" or "His steadfast love endures for-ever," ask the congregation to shout it back. Bring the music back up to full vol-ume as participants are seated. Then bring it down for the next segment.

Offering

Leader: As we offer our abundance to others today, let us remember the true sustenance that Jesus offered at the Feast of Booths—"Let anyone who is thirsty come to me, and let the one who believes in me drink" (John 7:37-38).

Use "What gift can we bring" (see Resources for This Festival) or other offertory hymn for instrumental music as the offering is collected. Also use this time to bring the food baskets to the *sukkah*.

Rain and Water Celebration

Find the reading of psalms in the "Psalm Collage" from the resource section for this festival. As the readers read these psalms using weather images, gently tilt one or more rain sticks back and forth or play recorded sounds of a rainstorm in the background. Arrange the readers in a striking composition by having some standing, some seated on stools, some seated on the floor. It is best if the pas-sages are memorized, but if read they should be so well known that the reader can make steady eye contact with the audience. When not reading, others on stage listen attentively to the person speaking.

Hymn

Sing verses 1 and 3 of "Hosanna, loud hosanna."

Prayer

Thank you God for constant care, faithful leading, streams of renewal, and provi-sion for our needs.

Resources for This Festival

Reading of the Faith History: Nehemiah 9:4-21

Readers 1-4: We give thanks unto you, O Lord our God!

Reader 1: Blessed be your glorious name, which is exalted above all blessing and praise.

Reader 5: You are the Lord, you alone;

Reader 2: you have made heaven, the heaven of heavens, with all their host, the earth and all that is on it, the seas and all that is in them.

Reader 6: To all of them you give life, and the host of heaven worships you.

Reader 3: You are the Lord, the God who chose Abram and brought him out of Ur of the Chaldeans and gave him the name Abraham; and you found his heart faithful before you, and made with him a covenant.

Reader 7: You have fulfilled your promise, for you are righteous.

Reader 4: And you saw the distress of our ancestors in Egypt and heard their cry at the Red Sea.

Reader 8: You performed signs and wonders against Pharaoh, and all his servants and all the people of his land, for you knew that they acted insolently against our ancestors.

Reader 1: You made a name for yourself, which remains to this day.

Reader 2: And you divided the sea before them, so that they passed through the sea on dry land,

Reader 3: but you threw their pursuers into the depths, like a stone into mighty waters.

Reader 4: Moreover, you led them by day with a pillar of cloud,

Reader 5: and by night with a pillar of fire, to give them light on the way in which they should go.

Reader 6: You came down also upon Mount Sinai, and you spoke with them from heaven.

Reader 7: You gave them right ordinances and true laws, good statutes and commandments.

Reader 8: and you made known your holy Sabbath to them and gave them commandments and statutes, and a law through your servant Moses.

Reader 2: For in their hunger you gave them bread from heaven,

Reader 4: and for their thirst you brought water for them out of the rock;

Reader 6: and you told them to go in and to possess the land that you swore to give them.

Reader 8: But they and our ancestors acted presumptuously and stiffened their necks and did not obey your commandments;

Reader 1: they refused to obey, and were not mindful of the wonders that you performed among them;

Reader 3: but they stiffened their necks and determined to return to their slavery in Egypt.

Reader 5: But you are a God ready to forgive, gracious and merciful, slow to anger and abounding in steadfast love,

Reader 7: and you did not forsake them.

Reader 6: Even when they had cast an image of a calf for themselves and said,

Reader 5: "This is your God, who brought you up out of Egypt,"

Reader 4: and had committed great blasphemies,

Reader 3: you in your great mercies did not forsake them in the wilderness;

Reader 2: by the pillar of cloud that led them in the way did not leaven them by day,

Reader 1: nor the pillar of fire by night that gave them light on the way by which they should go.

Reader 8: You gave your good spirit to instruct them,

Reader 2: and did not withhold your manna from their mouths,

Reader 7: and gave them water for their thirst.

Reader 4: Forty years you sustained them in the desert wilderness

Reader 6: so that they lacked nothing;

Reader 3: their clothes did not wear out

Reader 5: and their feet did not swell.

Readers 4-8: Stand up and praise the Lord your God, who is from everlasting to everlasting!

Rain and Water Celebration—a Psalm Collage

Reader 1: Sing to the Lord with thanksgiving; make melody to our God on the lyre. He covers the heavens with clouds, prepares rain for the earth, makes grass grow on the hills. (Ps.147:7-8)

All: Hosanna! [*All readers beat their willow sticks five times on the ground.*] Hosanna!

Reader 2: He turns a desert into pools of water, a parched land into springs of water. And there he lets the hungry live, and they establish a town to live in; they sow fields, and plant vineyards, and get a fruitful yield. (Ps. 107:35-37)

All: Hosanna! [*Beat willow sticks five times on the ground.*] Hosanna!

Reader 3: You visit the earth and water it; you greatly enrich it; the river of God is full of water; you provide the people with grain, for so you have prepared it. You water its furrows abundantly, settling its ridges, softening it with showers, and blessing its growth. You crown the year with your bounty; your wagon tracks overflow with richness. The pastures of the wilderness overflow, and the hills with joy, the meadows clothe themselves with flocks, and the valleys deck themselves with grain, they shout and sing together for joy. (Ps. 65:9-13)

All: Hosanna! [*All readers beat their willow sticks five times on the ground.*] Hosanna!

Reader 4: When the waters saw you, O God,

Reader 5: when the waters saw you, they were afraid;

Reader 4: the very deep trembled.

Reader 5: The clouds poured out water.

Reader 4: The skies thundered;

Reader 5: your arrows flashed on every side.

Reader 4: The crash of thunder was in the whirlwind;

Reader 5: your lightnings lit up the world;

Reader 4: the earth trembled and shook.

Reader 5: Your way was through the sea,

Reader 4: your path through the mighty waters;

Reader 5: yet your footprints were unseen. (Ps.77:16-19)

> **All:** Hosanna! [*All readers beat their willow sticks five times on the ground.*] Hosanna!

Reader 6: You make springs gush forth in the valleys; they flow between the hills, giving drink to every wild animal; the wild asses quench their thirst. By the streams the birds of the air have their habitation; they sing among the branches. From your lofty abode you water the mountains; the earth is satisfied with the fruit of your work. (Ps.104:10-13)

> **All:** Hosanna! [*All readers beat their willow sticks five times on the ground.*] Hosanna!

Reader 7: O God, you are my God, I seek you, my soul thirsts for you; my flesh faints for you, as in a dry and weary land where there is no water. (Ps. 63:1)

Reader 8: [*Standing*] On the last day of the festival, the great day, while Jesus was standing there, he cried out, "Let anyone who is thirsty come to me, and let the one who believes in me drink. As the scripture has said, 'Out of the believer's heart shall flow rivers of living water.' " (John 7:37-38)

> **All:** Hosanna! Hosanna! Hosanna! [*All readers wave their palm branches in the air.*]

What gift can we bring

ANNIVERSARY SONG 11 11. 11 11

Unison

1 What gift can we bring, what pres - ent, what to - ken? What
2 Give thanks for the past, for those who had vi - sion, who
3 Give thanks for to - mor - row, full of sur - pris - es, for
4 This gift we now bring, this pres - ent, this to - ken, these

words can con - vey it – the joy of this day? When grate - ful we come, re-
plant - ed and wa - tered so dreams could come true. Give thanks for the now, for
know - ing what - ev - er to - mor - row may bring, We're giv - en God's word that
words can con - vey it – the joy of this day! When grate - ful we come, re-

mem - b'ring, re - joic - ing, what song can we of - fer in hon - or and praise?
stud - y, for wor - ship, for mis - sion that bids us turn prayer in - to deed.
al - ways, for - ev - er, we rest in God's keep - ing and live in God's love.
mem - b'ring, re - joic - ing, this song we now of - fer in hon - or and praise!

Words and Music: Jane Marshall

How Fantastic!
Celebrating Epiphany

3

The most beautiful thing we can experience is the mysterious.
It is the source of all true art and science.
—Albert Einstein

Epiphany traditionally celebrates the visit of the magi to the Christ child. In the early church, it was a time to celebrate the baptism of Christ. In a broader sense, Epiphany is defined as a manifestation of the divine, hence the birth of Jesus is an epiphany. Generally, an epiphany is an experience in which a person suddenly perceives the essential nature of something through a simple, yet striking, event. Our celebration today exalts the simple, yet striking, manifestation of God in Christ's birth and in our own day.

Bible Text

Matthew 2:1-18

Bible Background for Our Celebration

Epiphany is also known as the Twelfth Day of Christmas and marks the climax of the Christmas season. The Western concept of Epiphany focuses on the visit of the magi. This was the first manifestation of Christ to the Gentiles. The magi were foreign astrologers, the scientists of the day and also interpreters of dreams. In their normal routine, they were open to the mysterious calling of God. They saw a star and followed with abandon to search for a new king, to worship him and offer gifts.

Epiphany is a time to celebrate the fantastic and mysterious ways in which God

works. By means of a bright star, God beckoned the magi to visit the Christ child, which is fantastic enough. But these were Gentiles, outsiders, a people excluded from God's family. That God would give the magi a key role in the drama of Christ's birth is even more fantastic. God spoke to the magi in a dream warning them not to return to Herod. It is equally striking that the magi heeded his warning with such confident action. Some say that these details point to the early church's conviction that the coming of Christ had universal significance. This King was not just the King of the Jews!

Faith Nugget

God continues to act in mysterious and unusual ways in our day.

Early Preparation

Convene a planning committee a month ahead of time. Select a worship leader, soloist, accompanist, and someone to tell a children's story. Also arrange for leaders for each discussion and reflection group.

At least four weeks ahead, select the cast (Mary, a baby or young child, three magi, Herod) for the drama. The drama is entwined with other components of the celebration. It is vital that each actor knows exactly what is going to happen next. Practice twice with scripts so movements can be written in. Then practice at least twice after actors have memorized the script.

Construct a sign shaped like an arrow that says PALACE. Use heavy cardboard or plywood. Cover it with aluminum foil or glittery paint. With a utility knife, put two-inch slits around the perimeter. Lay a strand of blinking Christmas lights on top of the sign, stuffing the wiring into the slits, front to back. You may want to put more than one light at each slit. Cut large block letters for the word PALACE from construction paper and place the word in the center of the arrow. Make it as flashy as possible. Hang the sign so the arrow points to an exit from the area. Herod will be unseen as he delivers his lines.

Gather props for the drama and hang a star over the area where Mary sits. The star should be large and well lighted either by a bulb in the center of it or by a spotlight.

Purchase magic gadgets from a novelty store or theater supply store in plenty of time for the storyteller to practice. A stick that becomes a flower and a scarf that changes color are two tricks that are easy to master and are fairly inexpensive.

Gather materials to make luminaries during the celebration.

You will need

- ❏ a slip of paper to be placed in each bulletin, which reads: To you, O Christ, I offer the gift of_____.
- ❏ a large star that blinks or has a spotlight on it
- ❏ PALACE sign materials: a large cardboard arrow, a string of Christmas lights, aluminum foil, utility knife, construction paper
- ❏ props: gifts to carry, bows to place on the gifts, map, baskets for offering, camera on a neck strap, baby or child
- ❏ costumes: traditional biblical robes for Mary, Christ child, and magi
- ❏ magic gadgets for children's story
- ❏ luminaries: empty soft drink cans, kitchen scissors, black and white spray paint, newspapers, ice pick or nails, hammers, votive candles, matches
- ❏ nature videos or pictures

Name of your church

How Fantastic!

Celebrating Epiphany

Gathering

Opening Hymns.................."He leadeth me"

Call to Worship [*stand*]

Epiphany Centers
1. Dreams in the Bible
2. Human Rights for Children
3. Journals
4. Luminaries
5. God's Mysteries
6. Christian Illusionist

Time with the Children

Drama ...."The Wise Guys," Part 1

Hymns ...."As with gladness men of old"
"We three kings"

Drama ...."The Wise Guys," Part 2

Hymn....."O come, all ye faithful" (vv. 1-2)

Offering
Solo ...."What gift can we bring"
Prayer of Dedication for Gifts

Mary's Song ....Luke 1:46-55

Hymn ..."The virgin Mary had a baby boy"

Drama ...."The Wise Guys," Part 3

Hymn ...."Lord, you sometimes
speak in wonders"
"Open our eyes, Lord"

Sending

The Celebration

Gathering

Give the meeting place an atmosphere of celebration. White is the traditional color of Epiphany, and typical decorations include angels, the magi, and images of the Christ child. As people are arriving, play traditional Christmas carols.

Hymn

Sing "He leadeth me" or another hymn about God's guidance.

Call to Worship

All: Come, let us celebrate! Let us celebrate God who works in mysterious and fantastic ways.

> **One:** God beckoned to the magi with a star.
>
> **All:** How incredible!
>
> **One:** God gave the magi key roles in the drama of Christ's birth, even though they were Gentiles.
>
> **All:** How outrageous!
>
> **One:** By speaking to them in a dream, God told the magi not to return to Herod.
>
> **All:** How mysterious!

Leader: God continues to act in incredible, fantastic, and mysterious ways.

> **All:** Let us be open to hear and follow God's divine direction. Amen.

Epiphany Centers

Give brief instructions for dismissal to Epiphany activity centers. Ask everyone to choose one center from the list in the bulletin. Each center helps to define or experience Epiphany in some way. Instruct people to return to the gathering place when they hear music.

1. Study Dreams in the Bible. Use a concordance to find the many accounts of dreams. Also look up the terms *vision* and *of the Spirit*: Ezekiel 8:3; 11:24; 40:2; Matthew 1:20; Matthew 2:12, 19, 22; Luke 1:22; 2 Corinthians 12:1; Acts 2:17. In 1 Samuel 28:6, three ways are listed for knowing the mind of God: dreams, *Urim* (sacred lot), and prophets. Focus on the dream material in Genesis or the visions in Revelation. What insights can they give us? What new information is given in Numbers 12:8? God came to people in the Bible in a personal way through dreams, visions, and angels. Give modern examples of God speaking in dreams and visions. Tell what revelations you have received from God in dreams.

2. Learn About Human Rights for Children. The story of Epiphany is not complete without reading Matthew 2:16-18, which focuses on Herod's fear of losing power. So intense was the threat posed by the infant King that Herod ordered the slaughter of children under the age of two in Bethlehem and surrounding areas to eliminate all possible contenders for Herod's throne. God is with us in the face of evil and in the midst of pain and suffering. Why do we usually omit this part of the Christmas story? Make a list of areas in the world where children are being killed or hurt today. How is God with them? Discuss times when God has been with you in your pain, and celebrate God's presence. Also list those people in your congregation who are in pain and need to feel God's presence. End with a time of prayer for all these people.

3. Write in a Journal. This group needs a quiet space. Appoint a convener who can gather the group and get them started. Perhaps begin by singing "Open my eyes, that I may see." Give out the statement, Bible verse, and questions listed below to each participant as food for thought. Then allow the group to reflect quietly and keep a journal if they so desire. Near the end of the allotted time, ask if anyone would like to read from or tell about his or her journal.

God's Ways Are Fantastic. Be Aware!
Reflect on Isaiah 55:8-9. Then ask yourself these questions:
• What keeps you from seeing "unbelievable" signs from God?
• How can we better tune into God's higher ways?
• God did not come to us in Jesus with the power we expect from kings. What surprising ways have you seen God's power in your life?
• In what ways have you seen God's work through dreams?

4. Make Luminaries. As God used the star to guide the magi to Jesus, so we are to be a light to the world, pointing others to Christ. Consider the advice in Philippians 2:14-15: "Do all things without murmuring and arguing, so that you may be blameless and innocent, children of God without blemish in the midst of a crooked and perverse generation, in which you shine like stars in the world."

To remind us of our calling, make luminaries to shine in the dark. Give each person a clean tin can or aluminum soft drink can (cut off the tops of the cans with kitchen shears). Spray paint the cans black. When the paint is dry, pack the cans tightly with newspapers to keep their form while you poke holes in the side of the can in the shape of a star. This can be done with a hammer and a nail or with an ice pick. Some cans are so thin a ballpoint pen will do the job. Place a votive candle in the luminary. Display the luminaries in the celebration. If candles present a fire hazard, set the cans over the bulbs of a string of white Christmas lights.

5. Look at God's Mysteries in Our World. God's inventive and mysterious powers often are revealed in nature. Memorize one or more verses of Psalm 8. Then show a portion of a video on natural history showing God's wonders. Ask what the handiwork of God tells us about God.

6. Watch a Christian Illusionist. Invite an illusionist who uses his or her tricks to teach Christian truths. Let each person master a trick, such as the scarf or flower trick used in the children's story.

Time with the Children

The storyteller invites children to come together while musicians provide a musical interlude of "He leadeth me." He or she will use this time to prepare children for the celebration of Epiphany and the drama that follows. The magic tricks are symbolic of actions we cannot comprehend. Don't leave children with the impression that God's works are magic.

The storyteller says something like this: The Bible tells us that God is much greater than we are. God does many things we cannot do, like creating the world and giving life to plants, animals, and people. Does it surprise you that One so powerful and great wants to talk with us and call us God's people? Well, God does surprising things at times, things we barely understand. Who else would think of turning a crawling caterpillar into a flying butterfly or a swimming tadpole into a jumping frog? Who would think that this stick could turn into a flower [*perform trick*] or that this red scarf could become a blue one [*perform trick*]. How did that happen? It's a mystery until you understand. Here is how it's done. [*Explain how one trick was done. Let the other remain a mystery.*]

When Christ came to the world as a baby, it was a big surprise to everyone. They thought the King would be a powerful, grown man. To the people who were waiting for a king, the news that the King was a baby was outrageous! It wasn't what they expected. It was a little like a magic trick that catches people off guard. Did you know that some of the first people to understand that Jesus was truly the King to save the world were magicians of sorts? We call them wise men or the magi. [*Actors enter. Keep children where they are.*]

The Wise Guys: Part 1

Actors perform Part 1 of the drama called "The Wise Guys" found in the resource section for this celebration.

Hymns

During this musical interlude, sing Epiphany carols, such as "As with gladness men of old" and "We three kings."

The Wise Guys: Part 2

The second part of the drama is continued as found in the resource section.

Hymn

Sing the first and second verses of "O come, all ye faithful."

Offering

Leader: As the wise ones offer their gifts to Christ, let us offer ours. We bring not only monetary gifts, but also gifts of time, abilities, possessions, and attitudes. As the soloist sings "What gift can we bring," pray about the gift you would like to offer to Jesus. Write your idea on the slip of paper in your bulletin. When you are finished writing, bring your idea forward and place your offerings, both monetary and written, in the baskets by the stable scene.

[*"What gift can we bring" is found on page 24. The accompanist will continue to play the song after the soloist finishes, until all in the congregation have given their gifts. As the last of the congregation give their gifts, the wise ones rise, move to another part of the stage, and recline to sleep.*]

Prayer of Dedication for Gifts

All: Our Dear Christ and Lord, to you we dedicate these gifts given from our pockets and our hearts. We pray that you might use them, and us, in wonderfully surprising ways. Amen.

Mary's Song

Mary, in the tableau, lifts her head in a prayer of thanksgiving, reciting Luke 1:46-55. This is memorized and recited as a monologue. Mary's song is usually part of the annunciation before Jesus' birth, but it is appropriate here because it gives thanks for God's surprising favor. Not only does God come to us as a weak infant, God delivers the infant King to a peasant woman. Everything about the birth of Jesus is surprising.

Hymn

Sing a carol about Jesus' birth, such as "The virgin Mary had a baby boy." Mary exits during the hymn.

The Wise Guys, Part 3

The drama continues as found in the resource section.

Hymn

Sing a hymn about God's presence, such as "Lord, you sometimes speak in wonders" or a chorus, such as "Open our eyes, Lord, we want to see Jesus"

Sending

All: Open our eyes that we may see you.
Open our ears, that we may hear you.
Open our time, that we may wait for you.
Open our minds, that we may understand you.
Open our hearts, that we may follow you. Amen.

Resources for This Celebration

The Wise Guys

Cast:

Wise person 1 is portly.

Wise person 2 is excited by new ideas.

Wise person 3 enjoys being a tourist.

Use traditional biblical period dress even though the drama makes references to modern life and uses modern props.

Part 1
[*A door bursts open loudly to surprise everyone. Wise guys enter, looking up and around, checking out the scenery.*]

3: Jerusalem! We're here at last! It's more beautiful than I expected! A perfect place for the King of Kings to live! [*He takes a photo of a congregation member.*] And such beautiful people!

1: That was a long journey.

2: Especially when you stop at every camel stop for a snack.

3: Which way to the new king, do you suppose?

1: Let's ask these intelligent looking children here [*approach the children*].

3: Oh, they're adorable! [*takes a photo*] Excuse me, we're new in town and we're looking for the king's house. Do you know how to get there? [*Children's story-teller holds up map.*]

2: Hey, a map. What a wise idea! [*They open it and look.*]

1: Hum . . .

2: Hum . . .

3: Hum . . .

1: [*pointing to map*] This must be the place. It says BURGER KING. [*asks children*] Is that the name of the royal palace? [*PALACE sign lights up.*]

3: [*pointing to the sign*] Hey, this looks like the way! We don't need that map!

1: Shall we proceed?

2: Wise idea.

3: Thanks, children! We're going to send you back to your parents now. Be careful. Watch out for our camels. They like to spit on people they don't know. Step carefully.

[*Children return to parents as wise men dust each other off, spruce up, put bows on their presents, and then head for the palace sign.*]

2: Wait. [*They stop.*] I wish we could see that incredible star just to be sure. Doesn't that look like a star over there?

3: That pale little thing? I think not. Let's head for the palace! [*takes photo of sign*]

2: Are you sure we're going the right direction? It's not wise to . . .

1: Look, we've come to worship the greatest King the world has ever known . . .

3: Will ever know.

1: Worship, my friend, happens best in great marble halls where they can hold great feasts!

3: Besides, look at all this camel traffic. If you kneel anywhere else, you might get into something you didn't expect. You wouldn't want to get anything nasty on your new robe would you?

2: No I suppose not, wise idea.

1: We've got gifts fit for a king . . .

3: And kings are in palaces. What do you expect? Come on.

2: I'm getting nervous. Maybe frankincense wasn't such a wise idea for a gift.

[*Exit to palace.*]

Part 2

[*This scene begins behind the closed palace door. Be sure to encourage actors to project so they can be heard. Herod is not seen by the audience.*]

Herod: [*in a roaring voice*] YOU'RE LOOKING FOR WHOm? [*voice suddenly becomes sweet and patronizing*] Oh, sit down and have a bagel and cheese while I consult with my advisors. [*All actors out of sight say "mumble, mumble, mumble, mumble, Bethlehem? mumble, mumble, mumble Bethlehem," to signify consultation.*]

[*The door opens.*]

Herod: [*calling in sickeningly sweet voice*] Be sure to come back now!

[*Wise men come out and stand by door.*]

3: No new king there.

2: That place gave me the creeps.

1: [*licking fingers*] It left a bad taste in my mouth, too.

2: It would have been wise to look for the star.

3: Bethlehem is the place to go, they said. [*pulls out map*] We could take the bypass or go on the throughway and see the city. What do you think?

2: I have no idea which would be best. If only we could see the star to be sure.

[*They slowly walk across the room; 3 is still consulting the map; 2 keeps scanning the sky. The palace sign goes out. The star lights up. Mary and baby move on stage and sit under star.*]

2: [*sees star*] Hey, look. [*They cross back to front near Mary and child. They look around a bit uncomfortably. Then they confer.*]

1: This must be the place.

2: Well, it's not quite what I expected! I had no idea we'd find the new King in such ordinary surroundings.

3: It's a surprise, that's for sure.

1: But when we followed the usual directions, we ended up in the wrong place. Now we're following the sign God gave, so it must be right.

2: Wise thinking.

3: Let's go nearer. What a lovely sight. [*takes photo*]

[*While congregation sings, wise guys offer gifts, kiss the baby, take photos, and kneel carefully to form a tableau to be sustained during the offering.*]

Part 3
[*All awaken.*]

1: Whew! That's the last time I eat bagels! I just had the worst nightmare. Something about Herod killing babies.

3: Really? I just had a nightmare about the same thing!

2: Uh, oh! So did I. I think it'd be a wise idea to pay attention to this dream.

Herod: [*offstage, banging on the palace door*] WHERE ARE THEY?!

3: I think I've seen all I want to see of Jerusalem. Let's take the scenic route through the country this time.

2: Wise idea!

3: [*as they gather up belongings for the return journey*] What a surprising trip this has been! Who would think that the King we came to see would be an innocent child and in such a place. [*takes a photo of the spot where they met the child*]

1: And who would think that God would lead us to honor him when he has so many followers right here.

2: I'm surprised we all dreamed that King Herod dream.

1: Hey, I'm hungry.

3: Now that's no surprise!

2: I really do think we ought to get going.

Herod: [*offstage, a banging door*] BRING ME THOSE MAGI! WHERE'S THAT BABY?

2: And I think we ought to go fast.

1 and 3: Now there's a wise idea!

[*They exit swiftly opposite the palace.*]

The Gift of Freedom

Celebrating Seder

4

Where the Spirit of the Lord is, there is freedom.
—*2 Corinthians 3:17*

Children ask questions. And one of the most common questions children ask their parents is, Why? It is their way of trying to make sense out of the world in which they live. In the religious realm, the Passover celebration encourages children, and adults for that matter, to ask faith questions and to learn by example. Their questions lead to stories and rituals that explain the past and involve people in the same search their ancestors undertook for understanding. In Exodus 13:14, Moses said, "When in the future your child asks you, 'What does this [the Passover] mean?' you shall answer, 'By strength of hand the Lord brought us out of Egypt, from the house of slavery.'" Reenacting the meal and asking the questions bring us all in touch with the saving work of God in our own lives. God commanded the Israelites to celebrate the Passover so that neither the experience of slavery nor the story of how God delivered them would be forgotten. If we do not remember the depths of pain, it is hard to grasp the heights of joy.

The Passover is a seven-day Jewish festival that celebrates freedom and redemption. On the first evening of Passover, the Seder meal and ritual are celebrated. This ritual meal is a time of remembering how God redeemed the Israelites from slavery into freedom and made them God's people. The freedom is tied to the covenant relationship with God.

The Seder, which means order, is a way of reliving the story of the Exodus through symbols, story, and song. Celebrants at the Seder are encouraged to make the Israelites' story their own story, for as we feel the pain and bitterness of slavery, the joy of God's saving acts takes on new meaning.

By celebrating the Seder here, we do not intend to make it a Christian holiday. Rather, as we learn more about the Seder's rich tradition, we grow in our understanding of God's redeeming activity. We are familiar with the Lord's Supper, which was possibly a Seder meal, but our understanding of the bread and the cup is deepened when we learn the context in which Jesus said, "This is my body, which is given for you. Do this in remembrance of me," and "This cup that is poured out for you is the new covenant in my blood" (Luke 22:19-20).

The final part of this celebration contains a feetwashing service and the Lord's Supper. In John, it is recorded that Jesus performed the symbolic act of feetwashing and said, "For I

have set you an example, that you also should do as I have done to you. . . . If you know these things, you are blessed if you do them." The first Lord's Supper would have been enacted during the Passover season. Putting Communion in this context adds a richness to its symbolism that we cannot understand otherwise.

By journeying through this time of remembrance, may we grow in our understanding of the Jewish liturgy and how God has redeemed us through Christ.

Bible Text

Exodus 12:24-28; 13:3-16; Deuteronomy 6:20-25; Matthew 26:17-19, 26-29; Mark 14:24; Luke 22:20; John 1:36; 13:1-17; 1 Corinthians 11:23-26; 1 Peter 1:17-23.

Bible Background for Our Festival

Passover is one of the Jewish festivals used to remember God's actions in history. It remembers a time when the Hebrews were slaves, and it reminds their descendants how God protected the Hebrews and "passed over" their homes during the tenth plague, the death of the firstborn child. In the exodus from Egypt, Jews smeared a lamb's blood on their doorposts to signify a Hebrew household so God would recognize the homes of Hebrews and "pass over" them, sparing them from the plague.

Passover began as a temple festival. A *Pesach* (Passover) lamb was killed in the temple on the eve of the Passover. It was to remind people of what the Hebrews experienced. After the Diaspora, the Passover was celebrated in the family home and the synagogue, and over time,

prayers replaced the sacrifices. Jews serve the Seder meal on the first night of Passover. The shank bone of a lamb is used to symbolize the way God passed over the Hebrew slaves' homes in Egypt.

In the Christian faith, Christ is the Passover offering, sacrificed to save us. In the Gospel of John, John the Baptist proclaims Jesus as the Lamb of God. Christ's death is also described as the death of the Passover lamb in 1 Peter 1:17-23. Christ was without defect, which was a requirement for the animal chosen to be the Passover lamb (Exod. 12:5). John states we have been passed over because Chris is the *pesach* lamb for us. As we share in the breaking of the bread, we remember what Jesus did for us.

In the Synoptic Gospels, it is noted that Jesus shared the Lord's Supper with his disciples and the cup is interpreted as the sign of the new covenant. This is also found in 1 Corinthians 11:23-26. The covenant made on Mount Sinai was sealed with the blood of the animal. Jesus' blood sealed a new covenant that all people might celebrate freedom and eternal life. Through Jesus all people can become God's people. Through the drinking of the grape juice, we remember how Jesus gave up his life that we might be a part of the new covenant.

Learning about what the Passover meal entails gives more meaning to the radicalness of Jesus' statements and our understanding of his death.

Faith Nugget

As God freed the Israelites from slavery, so through Christ we are saved from sin. Let us celebrate the gifts of freedom!

Early Preparation

In preparation for this celebration, form committees to plan and prepare the meal and to assemble decorations. Assign the program to a third committee. For the first meeting, six to eight weeks in advance, have all three committees present. Remember that though each committee meets separately to organize specific details, they each will need to coordinate their planning with each other. The food committee will plan both the symbolic Seder meal and a full meal to eat after the symbolic foods are eaten. The second meal does not need to be the traditional Seder foods.

The Seder meal is a distinctive celebration. Effort should be made to make the place where it is held special. Everything that is done at the Seder symbolizes the journey from slavery to freedom. For example, have some people sit at low tables, lounging on large pillows. In ancient Egypt only the free people were able to sit in such a way. The slaves had to eat standing for they were always at work. Consider putting a pillow on each chair to symbolize the freedom from slavery. Or put an announcement in the bulletin two weeks before the festival asking everyone to bring a pillow. Use the finest tablecloths you have.

Traditionally, preparations for the Passover begin with cleaning the house. In this ritual housecleaning, everyone searches for all the leavened bread in the house, for this food is banished from the home during the seven days of Passover. In Exodus 13:3, God tells Moses that one of the requirements of the commemoration is to refrain from eating anything containing yeast during Passover. Instead, *matza* (unleavened bread) is eaten during Passover. This symbolizes the haste in which the Hebrew people had to leave Egypt.

The food committee will need to make or buy unleavened bread. You will need a special plate on which to place three *matza* for the head table. Cover the *matza* with a fine napkin. It is customary to fold the cloth like an accordion, placing a single piece of bread in each of three folds. Leave enough fabric to cover the whole stack. On the other tables, place *matza* so it is available to all.

The Seder plate is near the leader's place. This is a large ornate plate that holds the five foods symbolizing the flight of the Hebrews. These foods include a roasted lamb bone, a roasted egg, sprigs of parsley, coarsely ground horseradish, and the combination of chopped apples, cinnamon, nuts, and grape juice. Beside every person's plate is a smaller plate with the following foods: ground lamb, a slice of a hard boiled egg, coarsely ground horseradish,

a sprig of parsley, and the combination of chopped apples, cinnamon, nuts, and grape juice.

The cup of Elijah is set by the plate of the leader. This is to be a special, beautiful cup. Elijah is a favorite prophet. This cup symbolizes the fifth promise of redemption, the hope in the kingdom of God coming.

At the head table, set an extra place. This is to remind us that our own freedom is incomplete until all people are free. The message of the Passover includes the struggle to preserve and advance the cause of freedom for all.

At each place setting is a wine glass, even at the children's places. It is acceptable to use grape juice. Each participant will drink from the cup four times. The number four is symbolic of the four promises of redemption that God made to Moses. Salt water is set in bowls to which everyone has access. This symbolizes the tears shed by the Jewish slaves.

The *Haggadah*, which means "story" or "to tell" in Hebrew, is read during the Seder. The story tells the saga of the people from the period of their slavery to their freedom. Purchase *Haggadah* booklets or borrow one from the library for the leader to use. Also print an order of service for each participant. This will include the responsive readings. It is not necessary to include explanations by the leader.

There are four questions built into the order of the Seder ritual, signifying that each person has the freedom to ask questions. These questions are typically asked by four children. Ahead of time assign four children to ask these questions, and assign four adults to respond to these questions.

Choose a leader for the festival. He or she needs to become familiar with the order and movement of the Seder. Ask a song leader to be responsible for choosing hymns and songs for the Seder.

Assign four people to perform a readers theater. One is the narrator, one male to be person A, and two females to be persons B and C. Give the script to them at least two weeks in advance. Have them practice two or three times together. The readers should know their parts well enough that they can look up from the page when they read their parts and do simple movements in character.

Make sure each family or household gets a written invitation to the Seder. You may want to ask for responses so you know how much food to prepare.

Assign one person to be a host at each table. This person will be responsible for starting the cloths and towels for hand-washing and making sure "wine" glasses are filled.

Find enough basins to place one at both ends of each table for feetwashing. Each basin is filled with warm water. Several towels and one chair are placed by each basin.

Prepare small loaves of bread and pitchers of grape juice for the Lord's Supper. Participants will drink the grape juice from the cups used during the Seder. Hosts will make sure cups are filled at the right times.

You will need

❏ three committees: food, decorations, and program
❏ invitations
❏ a Seder plate and Elijah's cup
❏ *matza* and fine napkins
❏ tables set with fine table cloths and two candles
❏ a head table
❏ an empty chair at the head table
❏ a place setting for each person
❏ "wine" glasses and grape juice
❏ a copy of the *Haggadah* at each place setting
❏ a copy of the order of service for everyone
❏ bowls of salt water
❏ pillows on each chair (have each person bring a pillow)
❏ a main meal (to be decided by the food committee)
❏ a person to lead the Seder
❏ four people for the reader's theater
❏ three or four people to lead singing
❏ four children to ask questions and four adults to respond
❏ a designated host at each table
❏ wet cloths and dry towels for hand-washing
❏ basins and towels for feetwashing
❏ a pillowcase
❏ a storyteller
❏ bread for the Lord's Supper

Name of your church
The Gift of Freedom
Celebrating Seder

Welcome

Order of the Passover Seder

Candlelighting
1. Kiddush: The blessing of wine
   The first cup of "wine"
2. Urehatz: Washing of the hands
3. Karpas: Eating a green vegetable
4. Yachatz: Break the middle matza: afikoman
5. Maggid: The Passover story
   The questions and answers
   "The Story of the Exodus"
   Hymn: ...."When Israel was in Egypt's land
   The plagues
   Song:................................"Dayenu"
   The three symbols
   The second cup of "wine"

6. Rahatz: Washing of the hands
7. Motzee-Matza: Blessing over the matza
8. Maror: Eat the bitter herb
9. Korekh: Eat the bitter herb and matza together
10. Shulhan Orekh: The Passover meal
11. Tzafun: The afikoman
12. Barekh: Grace after the Passover meal
    The third cup of "wine"
    The cup of Elijah
13. Hallel: Recital of the psalms
    Hymns of praise
14. Neertza: Conclusion of the Seder
    The fourth cup of "wine"

Monologue......................"The Lord Washes Peter's Feet"

Feetwashing

The Lord's Supper

Closing Song ...."Shalom, my friend"

The Festival

People enter and sit at tables. Reserve a seat at the head table for the leader. Leave a seat empty at the head table for Elijah. Encourage people to visit until the leader asks for everyone's attention.

Welcome

The leader enters dressed in a costume of Bible times. He or she then gives a description of the festival meal in which the congregation is about to take part: Welcome, welcome. I am so glad that you could come. What a glorious celebration Passover is. The Passover celebrates how God brought the Hebrew children out of slavery in Egypt and made them a free people. To get Pharaoh to let the Israelites go, God sent many plagues and hardships to the land of Egypt. The last plague was an angel of death who killed the firstborn in every household in the land. The Hebrews were told to put the blood of a special sacrificial lamb over the door of their houses so the angel of death would pass over and not stop at their houses. That is how this celebration got its name. We teach our children at Passover how God spared and freed us.

The journey you are invited to take tonight has symbols, stories, and songs that serve as a road map. We will travel through the pain and suffering of slavery to the joy and celebration of being a free people.

Through the ritual Seder meal that we celebrate tonight, the story becomes not just the story of our ancestors, but our story as well. We celebrate the freedom that is gained by God's saving grace. Yet, you will note the empty place at the table. We also acknowledge that we are not completely free until all people are free and able to join us at the table.

Let me tell you about what you see on the table before you. On the Seder plate, there is the shank bone of a lamb (*zeroah*). In Egypt, Hebrew slaves put the blood of the lamb on the top and sides of their door frames so that the Angel of Death would recognize Hebrew households and pass over their houses during the tenth plague. Later, Israelites remembered the story of their salvation by offering a lamb for sacrifice at the temple the night before Passover.

The egg is called *beytza*. It symbolizes rebirth and also the strength of the Jewish people.

Here are bitter herbs, called *maror* in Hebrew. When we taste this, we are reminded of the bitterness and hardship of slavery.

There is also the mixture of chopped apples, cinnamon, nuts, and wine, called *haroset*. This reminds us of the mortar that the Hebrews used when they were slaves in Egypt, forced to build cities.

The *karpas*, this piece of parsley, signifies springtime—the season of Passover. It is a sign for us of God's goodness to the earth.

Also on the table is salt water in which to dip the *karpas* (parsley). The salt water is used to symbolize the tears that the Israelites endured during their slavery.

On the second plate are three *matza*. The *matza* (unleavened bread) reminds us of the haste in which the Hebrews left Egypt. There was no time to let leaven work in the bread. Some see the three pieces as representing the three patriarchs: Abraham, Isaac, and Jacob. Later I will hide part of the middle *matza*. This piece is called the *afikoman*, meaning dessert. The children will look for it later in the celebration.

Each of us will drink four times from our own cup of grape juice. The four sips remind us of the four promises given by God to Moses. God promised to bring the slaves out of Egypt, free them from slavery, redeem them, and make them God's own people.

You will also notice this special cup, which is called the cup of Elijah. It is a symbol of hope for the coming of the kingdom of God.

Now it is time to experience the Exodus story for yourself. May its message of grace and redemption be as real in your life as it was in the lives of our ancestors.

The Order of the Seder
Candlelighting

Leader: To begin the Passover, we light two candles. The mother of the house or someone representing the mother usually lights them. *[Pause while the host at each table lights the candles.]*

Praised are you, O Lord our God, Ruler of the universe. Thank you, Lord of the light, for this opportunity to celebrate the Passover festival.

All: Praised are you, O Lord our God, Ruler of the universe. You have given us life, supported us, and empowered us to celebrate this time of freedom. *[Pause while the host at each table fills the wine glasses.]*

Kiddush (the blessing of the wine)
[People lift their cups while the leader offers a blessing.]

Leader: Blessed are you, our God, Sovereign of all, the One who created the fruit of the vine.

All: Praised are you, O Lord our God. In love, you have given us holidays for us to celebrate with jubilance. In remembrance of our liberation from Egypt, we celebrate this Feast of Unleavened Bread as you have commanded. You have given this feast of Unleavened Bread, the Season of Freedom, to commemorate our liberation from Egypt. Blessed are you, O Lord our God, who sanctified Israel and the festivals. *[All take the first of four drinks.]*

Urehatz (washing of the hands)
[One of the actors takes a pitcher and towel to the leader for the washing of hands.]

Leader: The second ceremony is known as *Urehatz*. The washing of hands is a symbolic act to prepare us for this sacred time. It illustrates our need for purification before we participate in the Seder. *[Leader pours water over each hand and dries both with the towel.]*

Karpas (eating a green vegetable)

Leader: In partaking of the *karpas*, we each dip the green vegetable into the salt water.

Praised are you, Ruler of the universe; we give you thanks for all the bounties of the earth which you give us. The salt water reminds us of the sweat and tears of the Hebrew slaves and all those still in slavery today. May we draw strength from the blessings which you give to ease the anguish of sorrow. Let us also remember those still in bondage, for our freedom is not complete while others are still suffering. *[Pause as people dip the karpas in salt water and eat it.]*

Yachatz (breaking the middle matza—the *afikoman*)

Leader: The *matza* is the unleavened bread. During the *yachatz*, I break the middle matza. Part of the broken piece of matza is left on the plate. The other half, the *afikoman*, I will hide. The children will search and find it after the dessert. The child who finds it will get a reward.

Maggid (the Passover story)
[The leader raises the plate with the three matza for all to see.]

Leader: The beginning of the *Haggadah* starts with "The Bread of Affliction," *Ha Lakhma Anya*.

All: This is the bread of affliction. It is a symbol of the haste in which the Israelites left Egypt, the land of slavery. It is also a symbol of the poverty and pain of many people today. It symbolizes the hope that all humankind may obtain freedom.

The Four Questions

[The children come forward or stand where they are to ask four questions.]

First child: Why is this night different from all other nights? On all other nights we eat leavened or unleavened bread. Why on this night only *matza*?

Second child: On all other nights, we eat herbs of any kind. Why on this night only bitter herbs?

Third child: On all other nights, we do not dip herbs even once. Why on this night twice?

Fourth child: On all other nights, our ancestors ate sitting or reclining. Why on this night did they all recline?

Leader: In response to your questions, I will tell you a story. Tonight is different for we celebrate being brought out of Egypt by God. If God had not acted on our behalf, we surely would still be deprived of freedom. The story gives us hope of freedom for all.

First adult: You ask why we eat unleavened bread this night. The *matza* speaks to the haste with which the Hebrews left Egypt. It tells in the Bible that the Egyptians told them to leave quickly because they were fearful they would all die. The Israelites did not put the yeast in the dough. Instead they took the dough as it was.

Second adult: You ask why we eat bitter herbs tonight. We eat bitter herbs to remember the night God passed over the Hebrew slaves' homes. On that night our Hebrew ancestors were commanded to eat bitter herbs. As we taste the bitter herbs, we are reminded of the cruel and painful existence of people living in slavery.

Third adult: You ask why we dip the greens twice tonight. First, we dip them in salt water to remember the tears of the slaves. Then we dip them in the *haroset,* which is the sweet mixture, to remind us of hope. It reminds us how the Israelites' tears of sorrow were transformed into tears of joy.

Fourth adult: You ask why we all recline tonight. In ancient times only free people were able to take the time to recline while eating. On this night the Israelites were freed, which we remember and experience by sitting in relaxed positions.

Leader: It is the duty of parents to tell the story of the Exodus to our children. On this night we hear and experience the story as if we were the Israelites. We join in their suffering from slavery, from being present during the plagues and from Pharaoh's hardened heart. Then we can understand the joy of being told we can leave the land of slavery. I invite you to enter into the story as if you were there.

The Story of the Exodus

Actors and a narrator deliver the dramatization of the Exodus story found in the resource section of this festival.

Hymn

Sing the traditional Passover song, "When Israel was in Egypt's land," sometimes called "Go down, Moses" (see Resources for This Festival).

The Ten Plagues

Leader: Moses and Aaron went before Pharaoh demanding that the Hebrew slaves be freed. Pharaoh would not listen. God sent ten plagues that caused much suffering for the Egyptians. As each plague is mentioned, everyone will dip the tip of their little finger in the grape juice and then take it out and drip a little grape juice on their plates. This symbolizes the emptying of our cups of joy as we remember the suffering of even our enemies.

All recite in unison:
Blood, Frogs, Vermin, Flies, Cattle disease, Boils, Hail, Locusts, Darkness, Slaying of the first born.

Song

Learn the traditional song "Dayenu," found in the resource section for this festival.

The Three Symbols

Leader: To remind us of the Exodus story just told, we eat symbolic amounts of the paschal lamb, unleavened bread, and bitter herbs, but in ancient times, the meal would have consisted primarily of these foods.

What is the *Pesach*? [*pointing to the roasted shank bone*]

All: The *Pesach*, the Passover lamb, reminds us how God passed over the houses of the Hebrew slaves to spare them from the tenth plague.

Leader: What is *matza*? [*holding up the matza*]

All: The *matza* symbolizes the haste in which the Hebrews left, not even allowing the bread to rise.

Leader: Why do we eat *maror*, bitter herbs? [*pointing to the bitter herbs*]

All: The *maror* recalls the ruthlessness the Hebrew slaves endured. They never rested and were subjected to the taskmaster's punishment if they did not work fast enough or hard enough.

Second Cup of Wine (the cup of memory)

Leader: God redeemed our ancestors from slavery in Egypt but redeemed them in Spirit as well. God's power of salvation is remembered as we drink of the cup of memory. [*Raise the cup.*]

All: Blessed are you, O Lord our God, Ruler of the universe, who created the fruit of the vine. [*All drink.*]

Rahatz (washing the hands)

[*Someone brings a wet cloth and dry towel to the leader.*]

Leader: We are ready to enjoy the meal. Before we eat, let us recite the blessing together. Then we shall wash our hands.

All: Blessed are you, Oh Lord our God, who sanctified us with your commandments and commands us concerning the washing of the hands.

[*Hosts bring a wet cloth and dry towel to each table for all participants to wash their hands.*]

Motzee-Matza (blessing over the matza)

[*The leader breaks the top matza into pieces and distributes it to all.*]

Leader: Blessed are you, O Lord our God, Ruler of the universe, who brings forth bread from the earth.

All: Blessed are you, O Lord our God, Ruler of the universe, who sanctified us by your commandments and commanded us to eat of *matza*. [*Everyone eats.*]

Maror (eating of the bitter herbs)

Leader: We will now eat of the bitter herbs. It reminds us of the bitterness of slavery. The *haroset* symbolizes how slavery can be sweetened by God's redemption [*dips the herbs in the haroset*].

All: Blessed are you, O Lord our God, Ruler of the universe, who make us holy by your commandments and commanded us to eat of bitter herbs. [*Everyone dips the herbs and eats.*]

Korekh (eating the bitter herbs and the *matza* together)

[*The leader instructs each participant to break off a piece of matza, which is then broken into two pieces. Place some bitter herbs between them to form a sandwich. All wait for the blessing before eating.]*

Leader: Hillel, a revered sage, observed the biblical commandment concerning the eating of the *Pesach* with *matza* and *maror*. In the Bible it is stated, "They shall eat the Passover offering together with *matza* and *maror*" (Num. 9:11). *[Pause as all eat. At this time the leader should hide the afikoman. A pillowcase is a common hiding place.]*

Shulhan Orekh (the Passover meal)
[The full dinner is now served. Allow people to eat leisurely and visit in a festive atmosphere.]

Tzafun (the afikoman)

Leader: Now is the time for the children to look for the *afikoman*. Whoever finds it will receive a reward.

[Young participants search for the afikoman. The award is given to the finder and the matza is broken and distributed for all to take a piece. Songs can be sung during this time.]

Leader: *Afikoman* means dessert. We will now partake of a piece of *afikoman*, making it the last thing we eat. *[All eat a piece of afikoman.]*

Barekh (grace after the Passover meal)

Leader: In Deuteronomy 8:10, we are commanded to say a grace after we have eaten: "When you have eaten and are satisfied you shall thank the Lord your God for the good land which he has given you."

All: Praise be to God, who is sustainer and giver of all good things.

The third cup (the cup of redemption)
[Hosts make sure the cups are filled.]

Leader: God's redemption is stated in Exodus 6:6: "I will redeem you with an outstretched arm and with mighty acts of judgment."

All: Blessed are you, O Lord our God,

Ruler of the universe, creator of the fruit of the vine. *[All drink.]*

The Cup of Elijah

Leader: Jewish tradition is that Elijah, the prophet, will precede and announce the Messiah who will bring freedom and peace for all people. We now welcome Elijah, beloved guest, at our Seder. Please rise. *[All stand. A designated person opens a door for Elijah. The cup of Elijah is filled and placed in the middle of the head table.]*

All: Let us remember with reverence all people who have suffered and perished from evil and persecution.

Leader: Let us remember the six million Jews killed in Europe. *[Pause for a moment of silent reflection.]* Others are suffering today because of their religious and spiritual beliefs. May their faith be an inspiration to us all. You may be seated.

Hallel (recital of the Psalms)
[Selected readers recite any praise Psalms between 113-118. Begin with a responsive rendition of Psalm 113.]

One: Praise the Lord.

All: Praise, O servants of the Lord, Praise the name of the Lord.

One: Let the name of the Lord be praised, both now and forevermore.

All: From the rising of the sun to the place where it sets, the name of the Lord is to be praised.

One: The Lord is exalted over all the nations, his glory above the heaven.

All: Who is like the Lord our God, the One who sits enthroned on high, who stoops down to look on the heaven and the earth?

One: He raises the poor from the dust and lifts the needy from the ash heap; he seats them with princes, with the princes of their people.

All: He settles the barren woman in her home as a happy mother of children.

Praise the Lord.

Hymn

Sing one or two hymns of praise.

Neertza (conclusion of the Seder)

[*Hosts should make sure that wine cups are filled for the Cup of Hope and Freedom.*]

Leader: [*raising a wine cup*] This is the cup of freedom. It reminds us of the hopes, struggles, and dreams of those who are seeking freedom. We are called to witness to this precious gift, so all may know of it.

All: Blessed are you, O Lord our God, Ruler of the universe, Creator of the fruit of the vine. [*All drink.*]

Leader: Let us conclude our Passover Seder with the liturgical poem by Rabbi Joseph Tov Elem of the eleventh century.

All: May He inspire us to nobler living and draw us close to Him. May the battle-cry for all who seek freedom ever ring in our ears.

Monologue: "The Lord Washes Peter's Feet"

An actor dressed in clothing of Bible times stands up and begins speaking. Find his script in the resource section for this festival.

Feetwashing

The hosts bring basins of warm water into the hall, placing one at the head and foot of each table and a chair by each basin. People remove their shoes and find partners of the same sex. If there is an odd number, a group of three may work together. If there are people who would feel more comfortable removing their shoes outside of the space where the congregation is assembled, suggest a Sunday school room that may be used for such a purpose. While the congregation sings, pairs take turns going to the basin nearest them. One sits in the chair and places one foot in the basin of warm water. The other stoops or kneels, putting the towel in her lap. She then lifts the foot with one hand and cupping

the other hand scoops some water over the foot in a symbolic washing. Then the washer towels the first foot dry and places it on the floor beside the basin. The same is repeated with the second foot. Then the pair switches positions. After both have had their feet washed, they stand and shake hands or embrace, giving one another a holy kiss on the cheek, saying a blessing, such as "Christ be with you" or "God bless you richly." Leave the towel for the next pair. They then return to their seats, replace their shoes, and join in the singing until all are finished washing feet.

The song leader may initiate singing hymns and songs *a capella* and then ask for favorites from the congregation. During the last song, the hosts carry out the basins and towels. This is a solemn and humbling ceremony that reminds us we are to be servants to one another.

The Lord's Supper

A host brings a number of small loaves to the leader's table. Hosts at each table will make sure everyone still has some grape juice. Decide ahead of time how you will involve children in this part of the celebration. It may be your practice to let them observe without taking part in the elements. Clarify for the children what they are to do.

Leader: On the night that Jesus was betrayed he took the bread and said, "This is my body broken for you, take and eat." [*Hosts go to the head table to get a loaf for their own table. At the table, each person takes off a piece and hands the bread to the next person. When everyone has bread, all eat.*]

Leader: In the same way, he took the cup. Please join me in lifting up your cups. Jesus said this is the sign of the new covenant, sealed with my blood, take and drink. [*All drink.*]

Closing Song

Sing a parting song, such as "Shalom, my friend."

Resources for This Festival

Drama: The Story of the Exodus

[*Cast: Narrator, and three readers (A,B,C)*]

Narrator: The time came when Joseph, a leader of the Hebrew people in Egypt, died. There was also a new pharaoh in power in Egypt. After some time the story of what Joseph had done for the people was forgotten and the Egyptians began to think of the Hebrews as a threat because of their great numbers.

A: Power, Power, I want more power.
I am the new pharaoh of the land.
Power, Power, I must never lose my power.

Who are all these Hebrew people?
How did they become so many?
Everywhere I turn, there they are.
Oh, this is not good.
What if they would rise up against me?
This is not good, they threaten my power.
What if another army came and they sided with them?
This is not good, there are too many of them.

I must deal with them cleverly.
They must not become more numerous.
They must never threaten my power.

Narrator: So, the Hebrews' pain began. First, he summoned the Hebrew midwives, Shiphrah and Puah.

B and C: Fret, Worry, Worry
Fret, Worry, Worry

C: What could he want from us?

B and C: Fret, Worry, Worry
Fret, Worry, Worry

B: Why would he summon us?

B and C: Fret, Worry, Worry
Fret, Worry, Worry

A: That is all we did until we came before him.

B: Yet nothing could have prepared us for what he commanded.

A: He commanded us to kill the male Hebrew babies when they were born.

A and B: No, No, No, we will not do it.
No, No, No, we can not do it.

A: We will tell him that the Hebrew women are not like the Egyptian women.

B: They are young and strong and have the babies before we get there.

Narrator: When Pharaoh realized that the Hebrews were continuing to multiply, he decided on a more drastic measure for their numbers needed to be decreased. All the male Hebrews under the age of two would be killed. The cries of the families could be heard across the land. There was a Hebrew woman who decided on a bold and daring plan.

A: Quickly, Miriam, Quickly,
we have no time to lose.
Quickly, Miriam, Quickly,
line the basket,
make it waterproof,
place your baby brother in it.
Let us hurry to the river. Yes, I hear the soldiers at the house next door. Let us go out the back. Place the basket on the river and may God protect him. Now, Miriam, stay in the reeds and watch over your baby brother.

B: Standing still in the reeds,
Standing still and watching.
Standing still in the reeds,
Standing still and watching.
There comes Pharaoh's daughter.
Oh no, the baby is crying.
Oh please stop, she will hear you.
Standing still in the reeds,
Standing still and watching.

Narrator: The Pharaoh's daughter heard the baby's cries;
she ordered her servants to quickly fetch the baby.
When she saw him, though she could tell he was
an Israelite baby, she claimed him as her own.

Miriam, seeing her chance, asked Pharaoh's daughter if she could get a wet nurse for her. She rejoiced as she went to get her mother.

Pharaoh was not satisfied, the Hebrews were continuing to increase.
He ordered the Hebrews to build him great cities.

A: Work, slaves, work,
you have no time to rest.
Work, slaves, work,
or the crack of the whip will be upon your flesh.
Work, slaves, work,

B: But I am old.

A: Silence, do what you are told.

C: But I am sick.

A: It does not matter. Work, slave, work.

Narrator: Moses grew into a young man. He saw the pain and suffering that his people endured. One day his anger was unleashed on an Egyptian who was beating a Hebrew. Moses killed the Egyptian. He ran for his life. He left the palace life he knew and went to the desert.

There he married and was a shepherd while his people continued to suffer deeply in Egypt. One day he saw a bush burning that did not seem to be consumed. As he came closer, the Lord spoke to him, saying,

"I am the God of your ancestors, the God of Abraham, the God of Isaac, the God of Jacob. I have indeed seen the misery of my people in Egypt. I have heard their outcry against their slave masters. I have taken heed of their suffering and have come down to rescue them from Egypt, and to bring them out of that country into a fine, broad land; it is a land flowing with milk and honey. The outcry of the Israelites has now reached me; yes, I have seen the brutality of Egyptians toward them. Come now; I will send you to Pharaoh and you shall bring my people Israel out of Egypt." Exodus 3:6-10

The Lord Washes Peter's Feet

My name is Peter. It was on a night like this that everything changed for me. Looking back, I can see that Jesus tried to prepare us for what happened, but we did not really want to hear, did not really want to understand. This was the man that we had left our family, friends, and home to follow. We had fears coming to Jerusalem because of the Jewish leaders not liking Jesus. But we put the fears aside when Jesus was received with such an overwhelming welcome. People heard that Jesus was coming and a great crowd assembled. It seemed like everywhere we looked, people were there. They were shouting, "Hosanna!" "Blessed is he who comes in the name of the Lord!" "Blessed is the King of Israel!" I can still hear the rustle of the palm branches being waved through the air and see Jesus riding through the crowd on a donkey.

During the evening meal, Jesus did something I did not understand. It was the task of each person to wash his or her own feet. After all the walking we did on the dusty road, our feet needed to be cleaned. On that night Jesus stood up and took off his outer clothing and then wrapped a towel around his waist. We all stared at him because we couldn't imagine what he was doing.

When he poured water in a basin, I thought, He isn't thinking of washing our feet, is he? But he did. He got down in front of John and washed his feet and dried them with the towel wrapped around his waist, not saying anything. Well, I was not going to just let this happen; when he came to me I asked, "Lord, are you going to wash my feet?" I just wanted a straight answer but you never got those from Jesus. He said that I did not realize now what he was doing, but later I would understand. I had enough of seeing Jesus act like a servant washing the other disciples' feet. He was our leader and teacher. I said no. "No, you shall never wash my feet." But then Jesus said, "Unless, I wash you, you have no part of me." Alright, so maybe I had been a bit hasty; I had been known to be that on occasion. I certainly did want to be a part of him so I said, "Not just my feet but my hands and my head as

well." Looking back I can see that Jesus was trying to prepare us for what was going to be happening, even though we couldn't comprehend it.

When he finished, he asked, "Do you understand what I have done for you?" I sure wasn't going to say anything this time. He continued by saying, "You call me Teacher and Lord and rightly so, for that is what I am. Now that I, your Lord and Teacher, have washed your feet, you also should wash one another's feet. I have set you an example, that you should do as I have done for you. I tell you the truth, no servant is greater that his master, nor is a messenger greater that the one who sent him. Now that you know these things, you will be blessed if you do them."

Later, when we understood things better, we began washing one another's feet. Oh, it was hard initially. For me, it was always easier to give than receive. So it was difficult allowing someone to wash my feet. On the outside, washing someone else's feet was an act of lowering oneself, however, it did not feel that way. We learned that to humble oneself was empowering. On the outside it would seem that the one having his or her feet washed would be exalted. Yet, it was humbling.

I did not understand that until I actually did it. I think that is why Jesus told us to follow his example. Jesus was not into power in the way the world understands it. By washing each other's feet, we got in touch with the way Jesus understands power. We are not made powerful by lording over others, but by humbly receiving and giving. We learned to understand what Jesus was trying to teach us. I have rambled on long enough and I want you to have the opportunity of washing each other's feet. Maybe it will help you understand what Jesus was trying to teach. It helped us in a new way.

When Israel was in Egypt's land

Irregular

1 When Is - rael was in E - gypt's land, let my peo - ple
2 "Thus saith the Lord," bold Mo - ses said, let my peo - ple
3 No more shall they in bond - age toil, let my peo - ple
4 The Lord told Mo - ses what to do, let my peo - ple
5 They jour - neyed on at God's com - mand, let my peo - ple
6 Oh, let us all from bond - age flee, let my peo - ple

1 go; op - pressed so hard they could not stand,
2 go; "If not, I'll smite your first - born dead,"
3 go; let them come out with E - gypt's spoil,
4 go; to lead the childr'n of Is - rael through
5 go; and came at length to Ca - naan's land,
6 go; and let us all in Christ be free,

let my peo - ple go. Go down, Mo - ses, 'way down in

E - gypt land. Tell old Phar - aoh, let my peo - ple go.

Text: African American spiritual
Music: African American spiritual

DAYENU

FOLK SONG

Da - da - ye - nu ___ da - da - ye - nu ___ da - da - ye - nu, da -

ye - nu, da - ye - nu, da - ye - nu   ye - nu, da - ye - nu.   *Had he brought us out of E - gypt*

And not fed us in the des - ert,   Brought us out of E - gypt, Well then — Da - ye - nu!

Had he fed us with the manna,
And not then ordained the Sabbath,
Fed us with the manna, well then—Dayenu!
Refrain

Had he then ordained the Sabbath,
And not brought us to Mount Sinai
Then ordained the Sabbath, well then—Dayenu!
Refrain

Come, Holy Spirit
Celebrating Pentecost

The forgiveness of God is the foundation of every bridge from a hopeless past to a courageous present.
—*George Adam Smith*

In the Gospel of John, we meet the disciples hiding behind locked doors after the crucifixion. The women had gone to the tomb and found it empty. The disciples were living in the reality that Jesus had died and now his body had been stolen. In John 20:9, it states that they did not understand that Jesus had been raised from the dead. Despite Mary Magdalene's proclaiming "I have seen the Lord," there was still fear and distrust among the disciples. Though Jesus had promised he would send the Comforter when he left, the disciples probably didn't even remember this message in the midst of their experience. If ever they needed a Comforter, they needed one now. In the midst of their terror, Jesus appeared, proclaiming "Peace be with you." To reveal to the disciples that he was indeed the risen Christ, Jesus showed them his scars. He breathed on them and said, "Receive the Holy Spirit. If you forgive the sins of any, they are forgiven them; if you retain the sins of any, they are retained." In so doing, he commissioned them to continue in the ministry he had begun.

At times we also find ourselves locked up. We might not be locked behind an actual door, but we are behind our own emotional armor. At times our dreams are shattered and we huddle together worrying about what will happen next. Whether we know it or not, we have not been left alone. The gift of the Holy Spirit brings us healing and empowers our ministry. We are called to proclaim the radicalness of God's forgiving nature. We are called to proclaim the good news.

Bible Text

John 14:8-17, 25-27; 15:26-27; 16:4b-15; 20:19-23

Bible Background for Our Celebration

Pentecost is the celebration of the outpouring of the Spirit on the early Christians. It is the climax of the Easter-Pentecost season and the culmination of God's promises in Jesus Christ. On Pentecost we remember and celebrate the sending of the Holy Spirit. It is a bittersweet memory—losing Jesus in order to have the Holy Spirit (John 16:7).

In the Bible the story of the giving of the Holy Spirit is told in two different ways. The Acts account is the more familiar version where the Holy Spirit comes as tongues of fire and in the sound of roaring wind.

The other account is found in John where Jesus appears to the disciples following his resurrection. He breathes on the disciples, giving them the Holy Spirit. The Interpreter's Bible notes that the term "the disciples" is inclusive of all who were around Jesus during his passion—men and women—not just the twelve disciples. He was not only giving them new life and power by the simple act of breathing on them, but also demonstrating that he was a resurrected living being, not simply an apparition. Breath is a sign of life.

The image of breath-giving life is also found in Genesis and Ezekiel. In Genesis 2:4-7, God forms a human being and breaths into him, bringing him to life. In Ezekiel a vast army is raised out of dry bones when life-giving breath is breathed on them. Jesus breathed on the disciples, showing the new life the Spirit gives.

The Pentecostal mission set forth in John focuses on forgiveness. Through the Pentecost we are given the mission to proclaim God's forgiveness. This is a valuable gift. Repeatedly in the Old Testament, God's forgiveness allows the people of Israel to be God's people. Over and over God forgives and draws the people near. In the New Testament, Jesus pronounces the sins of many and forgives them. The rulers who did not recognize the divinity of Jesus saw this as blasphemy and condemned him. As the body of Christ, we are commissioned to proclaim the need for forgiveness in this broken world.

Faith Nugget

We are not left alone in our fears; the Holy Spirit is with us, setting us free and empowering us to proclaim God's forgiveness to others.

Early Preparation

Four to six weeks ahead of time, select all the people you will need to carry out the celebration. Choose a storyteller and provide him or her with the story in the resource section for this celebration. Select a soloist to sing "Dry Bones" as part of the children's time. Assign people to lead activity centers and give them plenty of time to collect the materials they need. Appoint actors to perform a pantomime with music in the Music and Tableau presentation of John 20:19-23. The actors performing the pantomime should rehearse with the accompanist and quartet several times to be sure flow and timing are smooth. Invite a speaker to prepare a reflection on the topic suggested in the celebration.

You will need

- ❑ a copy of "Dry Bones" song
- ❑ a reader for "Dem Dry Bones" story
- ❑ gourds or bunches of keys to rattle, children to be bones and wind
- ❑ a soloist
- ❑ a quartet
- ❑ accounts of forgiveness
- ❑ a speaker on reconciliation
- ❑ a songleader
- ❑ breath mints
- ❑ rhythm instruments

Name of your church

Come, Holy Spirit
Celebrating Pentecost

Gathering ...."In thee is gladness"
"Come, thou, Almighty King"

Call to Worship

Prayers

Time with the Children .."Dem Dry Bones"

Pentecost Centers
1. Prayer for the Breath of God
2. Make Clay Figures
3. Learn About the Holy Spirit
4. Watch a Video
5. Breath Painting
6. Forgiveness and Reconciliation
7. Hymn-Sing About Forgiveness

Gather Again

Hymns ....."Breathe on me, breath of God"
"Spirit, come dispel our sadness"

John 20:19-23 in Music and Tableau

Quartet.........................."Holy Spirit, come
with power" (st. 1)
"Jesus, stand among us"

Litany of Confession

Hymns ....."Gracious Spirit, dwell with me"
"Spirit of the living God"

Offering

Quartet..."O Holy Spirit, by whose breath"

Reflections on Forgiveness

Responsive Hymn ...."I cannot dance,
O Love"

Benediction

Sending Hymn ...."Move in our midst"

The Celebration

Gathering

As people enter, hand each one a bulletin and sing two gathering hymns, such as "In thee is gladness," "Come, Thou almighty King," or "Spirit of God! descend upon my heart."

Call to Worship

One: Come, Holy Spirit, come.

All: In the midst of our fears and pain, come.

One: The disciples huddled together in the upper room.
Afraid to go out.
Jesus appeared.
He showed the marks on his hands and breathed on them.
The Holy Spirit came.

All: Breathe upon this congregation.
Scatter the darkness with your breath.
Infuse us with your life-giving Spirit.

Prayers

Leader: May this time of worship be life-giving for each person here. As gentle as a breath, the Spirit moves. May we be sensitive to the movement of the Holy Spirit moving among us. Inspire us. Heal us. Send us. Amen. [*Include prayers for members of the congregation or congregational concerns at this time.*]

Time with the Children

Introduce children to God's way of giving life through breath. For instance, when God created the first person, God formed the person out of clay and then breathed life into him. Then introduce children to Ezekiel and the dry bones that came to life with God's life-giving breath. Use the script, "Dem Dry Bones," in the resource section for this celebration.

Pentecost Centers

At the close of the children's time, dismiss the congregation to the Pentecost centers where they will focus on the life-giving breath of the Holy Spirit.

1. Pray for the Coming of the Breath of God. Read Philippians 4:6-7 aloud and then enter a time of silence. Suggest that participants reflect silently on the life and breath God has given them and how they are using life and breath to serve God. To be conscious of the life breathed into them, people may want to think about every breath they take for one or two minutes. Near the end of your prayer time, encourage people to reflect aloud any thoughts they want to share with the group. End by saying the Lord's Prayer together.

2. Make Clay Figures. In this group children and adults alike will use Play-Doh modeling compound to tell the story of creation. Have each person form a human being out of clay. Read the story from Genesis 2:4-7 of God creating Adam. Talk about how God breathed on the dust and it came to life. Also tell the story of the dry bones again. Then talk about how Jesus, the Son of God, breathed on the disciples, giving new life. Emphasize that the breath Jesus gave to the disciples is the Holy Spirit who is with us always. Note that the word *spirit* and *respirate* both mean "breath" in Latin.

3. Learn About the Holy Spirit. What are the characteristics of the Holy Spirit? What does it mean for us today to be filled with the Holy Spirit? Look up these various Bible passages and read them aloud.

Ezekiel 36:24-27; Luke 3:21-22; Luke 4:1-30; John 14:15-31; John 16:5-16; Acts 2; Acts 13:1-4; Acts 16:6-7; Acts 9:1-7; Ephesians 5:18; Romans 8:1-17; 1 Corinthians 2:6-16; 1 Corinthians 3:16-17. What insights do these passages give you about the Holy Spirit? Did you discover any connections or thoughts that are new to you? Where do you see the Holy Spirit at work today?

4. Watch a Video. Watch parts of a video, such as *Seeking the Lord* or *Dead Man Walking,* and talk about a ministry of forgiveness. Brainstorm actions you could take as a congregation or class to develop a ministry of forgiveness, such as prison ministry or shelter ministries.

5. Paint with Your Breath. Each participant selects poster paint in colors of their choice. Thin the paint slightly with water. Using a plastic spoon, place small pools of paint at several points around the edge of the poster board. Gently blow on the pools of paint to spread them. Lay paper flat to dry. Then with marker or paint, write "Breathe on me, breath of God" over this unique painted background. Post the paintings in the worship area.

6. Practice Forgiveness and Reconciliation. Invite a representative from a victim/offender reconciliation program to give a presentation to the group. The local police department may know of such groups in your area, particularly if they use them to lessen busy court schedules.

7. Sing About Forgiveness. Choose several songs about forgiveness and the Holy Spirit, and invite people to a sing-along. Have rhythm instruments available for participants to use. Choose one song for the group to sing for the whole congregation during the offering or after reflections.

Gather Again

People return to the gathering place when musicians begin playing or when recorded music is played.

Hymns

When most people are gathered, sing two Pentecost hymns, such as "Breathe on me, breath of God" and "Spirit, come, dispel our sadness," to set the stage for the following pantomime.

John 20:19-23 in Music and Tableau

A group of musicians and actors blend music and visuals to bring the scriptures to life in this portion of the celebration. The music suggested here is found in the resource section of this celebration.

Scene 1: Quartet sings verse 1 of "Holy Spirit, come with power" in double time.

Scene 2: Instrumentalists play through "Jesus, stand among us" one time as actors come forward and create a tableau of fearful disciples.

Scene 3: Quartet sings verse 1 of "Jesus, stand among us" as Jesus joins the disciples, showing them the scars on his hands and feet.

Scene 4: Instrumentalists again play softly through one verse of "Jesus, stand among us." Jesus says aloud, "Peace be with you! As the Father has sent me, I am sending you."

Scene 5: Quartet sings verse 2 while Jesus strikes a pose, breathing on the disciples.

Scene 6: Instrumentalists play through one verse again. Jesus says aloud, "Receive the Holy Spirit. If you forgive the sins of any, they are forgiven; if you retain the sins of any, they are retained."

Scene 7: Quartet ends by singing verse 3 of "Holy Spirit, come with power" in double time.

Litany of Confession

One: We confess that at times we also gather in fear,

All: Fear that paralyzes us,
Fear of the next knock of opportunity.
We confess that sometimes we do not recognize you.
Instead, we cling to fears that blind us.

One: Yet, you come to stand among us saying,
"Peace be with you."
With your scars we see the truth.
Death was defeated and victory reigns.

All: Jesus indeed did not leave us alone, we are not orphans.
The Holy Spirit is with us.
God be praised.

Hymn

Sing one or two Holy Spirit hymns, such as "Gracious Spirit, dwell with me" or "Spirit of the living God."

Offering

Leader: The Holy Spirit breathes new life into us to fit us for the work of reconciliation. Take a breath mint from the plate we are about to pass. Let it remind you of the breath of God at work among us. Then into the next plate that passes by, put in your offering. With our gifts we give new life and breath to our ministries. [*Quartet sings "O Holy Spirit, by whose breath"(see Resources for This Celebration) as children pass the mints and collect the offering.*]

Reflections on Forgiveness

Much of Christian faith centers on the forgiveness of sins—God's forgiveness of our sins. In the Gospel of John, Jesus gives us the ministry of forgiveness to carry on in his absence. Ask four or five people of different ages to tell about forgiving someone. Include, for instance, police officers, umpires and referees, school principals, business people, students, and parents. Or consider making an announcement several weeks ahead asking for anonymous stories of forgiveness and have readers read the accounts dramatically.

Responsive Hymn

Sing a hymn of response, such as "I cannot dance, O Love."

Benediction

Leader: Go, in the Spirit, walking in forgiveness.
Go, in the Spirit, proclaiming forgiveness.

Sending Hymn

Sing "Move in our midst," found on page 12.

Resources for This Celebration

Dem Dry Bones: Ezekiel 37:1-10

[This is a participatory story. Assign some children to be dry bones, lying on the floor. Assign a few others to rattle sets of keys or gourds when you tell them to, resembling the sound of dry bones. Another group of children can be wind, representing the entrance of the breath of God. Ask the congregation to join in on the chorus of "Dry Bones" when invited. Give each group a chance to try their part before the reader begins.]

The hand of the Lord came upon me, and he brought me out by the Spirit of the Lord and set me down in the middle of a valley; it was full of bones. *[Have the "bones" lie on the floor.]*

Congregation sings the chorus of "Dry Bones."

He led me all around them; *[reader walks among children lying on the floor]* there were very many lying in the valley, and they were very dry.

Congregation sings the chorus of "Dry Bones."

He said to me, "Mortal, can these bones live?" I answered, "O Lord God, you know." Then he said to me, "Prophesy to these bones, and say to them: "O dry bones, hear the word of the Lord."

Congregation sings the chorus of "Dry Bones."

"Thus says the Lord God to these bones: I will cause breath to enter you, and you shall live. I will lay sinews on you, and will cause flesh to come upon you, and cover you with skin, and put breath in you, and you shall live; and you shall know that I am the Lord."

Soloist sing the verses to "Dry Bones," stopping at thigh bones.

So I prophesied as I had been commanded; and as I prophesied, suddenly there was a noise, *[cue rattlers to begin rattling]* a rattling, and the bones came together, bone to its bone. I looked, and there were sinews on them, and flesh had come upon them and skin had covered them; *[poke one of the still children lying on the floor]* but there was no breath in them.

Soloist continues the song from hip bone to head.

Then he said to me, "Prophesy to the breath, prophesy, mortal, and say to the breath: Thus says the Lord God: Come from the four winds, O breath, and breathe upon these slain, *[cue breath to walk among the "bones," blowing gently]* that they may live."

I prophesied as he commanded me, and the breath came into them; and they lived and stood on their feet *[motion the "bones" to stand]*, a vast multitude.

Soloist sings "Dem bones, dem bones are going to walk around." Have the children with keys and gourds keep time with the music. Bring children and the whole congregation in on the chorus.

Jesus, stand among us

WEM IN LEIDENSTAGEN 65. 65

1 Je - sus, stand a - mong us in your ris - en pow'r.
2 Breathe the Ho - ly Spir - it in - to ev - 'ry heart.

Let this time of wor - ship be a hal - lowed hour.
Bid the fears and sor - rows from each soul de - part.

Text: William Pennefather, *Original Hymns and Thoughts in Verse,* 1873
Music: Friedrich Filitz, *Vierstimmiges Choralbuch,* 1847

Holy Spirit, come with power

BEACH SPRING 87. 87D

1 Ho-ly Spir-it, come with pow-er, breathe in-to our ach-ing night.
2 Ho-ly Spir-it, come with fi-re, burn us with your pres-ence new.
3 Ho-ly Spir-it, bring your mes-sage, burn and breathe each word a-new

We ex-pect you this glad ho-ur, wait-ing for your strength and light.
Let us as one might-y cho-ir sing our hymn of praise to you.
deep in-to our tir-ed liv-ing till we strive your work to do.

We are fear-ful, we are ail-ing, we are weak and self-ish too.
Burn a-way our wast-ed sad-ness and en-flame us with your love.
Teach us love and trust-ing kind-ness, lend our hands to those who hurt.

Text: Anne Neufeld Rupp, 1970
          Copyright © 1970 Anne Neufeld Rupp. Used by permission.
Music: attributed to B.F. White, *Sacred Harp*, 1844; harmonized by Joan A. Fyock
          Harmonization copyright © 1989 Joan A. Fyock. All rights reserved. Used by permission.

O Holy Spirit, by whose breath

ST. BARTHOLOMEW LM

1 O Ho - ly Spir - it, by whose breath life ris - es
2 You are the seek - er's sure re - source, of burn - ing
3 In you God's en - er - gy is shown. To us your
4 Flood our dull sens - es with your light. In mu - tual
5 From in - ner strife grant us re - lease. Turn na - tions
6 Praise our Cre - a - tor, Christ the Word, and praise the

1 vi - brant out of death, come to cre - ate, re - new,
2 love the liv - ing source, pro - tec - tor in the midst
3 var - ied gifts make known. Teach us to speak, teach us
4 love our hearts u - nite. Your pow'r the whole cre - a -
5 to the ways of peace. To ful - ler life your peo -
6 Spir - it, God the Lord, to whom all hon - or, glo -

1 in - spire. Come, kin - dle in our hearts your fire.
2 of strife, the giv - er and the Lord of life.
3 to hear; yours is the tongue and yours the ear.
4 tion fills; con - firm our weak, un - cer - tain wills.
5 ple bring, that as one bo - dy we may sing:
6 ry be both now and for e - ter - ni - ty.

Text: attributed to Rabanus Maurus, *Veni Creator Spiritus*, 9th c.; tr. John W. Grant, *Hymn Book*, 1971, alt.
          Copyright © 1971 John Webster Grant. Used by permission.
Music: Henry Duncalf, *Parochial Harmony*, 1762

The Many Ways of Faith 6

Celebrating Unity and Variety in Faith

> God is complete for himself, while for us he is continually being born.
> —*Pierre Teilhard De Chardin*

Every living thing on this planet needs the right environment to grow. Our faith life is no different. It is a living experience, changing and growing over a lifetime. Our community of fellow believers is the environment in which Christians can grow and expand in faith, share with others, and uphold each other in love. It is in this Christian environment that we see many ways of expressing belief and many levels of understanding as people move along on the journey of faith.

Christian educator John Westerhoff III has noted there are four distinctive styles of faith. He uses the illustration of a tree to explain the relationship between the different faith styles. First, each style is complete within itself. When a tree has one growth ring, it is just as much a tree as a tree that has eighty growth rings. The larger tree is not better but it is expanded. In a similar way, one style of faith is not better than another. People are not competing for a better faith, but they are seeking to expand their faith. Second, a tree needs the proper environment in order to grow, as a person does. If that environment does not provide the needed elements, a tree or a person will stop growing. Each tree, like a person growing in faith, grows in its own way and is unique. Third, a tree acquires more growth rings only by a slow, gradual process. The same is true for individuals growing in the faith. A person will not leap across faith styles but will acquire each one slowly and gradually. And finally, as a tree

grows, new layers encase the old growth. Old growth is not replaced. It is contained within. This is true for a person who is expanding in his or her faith. One style is not exchanged for another style. The new layer simply increases the old, encompassing it, building on it.

We celebrate our different styles of faith. God is present and constant in each of our journeys, no matter where we are. Our communities of faith are made up of many people at different places in their faith journeys. Let us celebrate our uniqueness as well as our similarities in faith styles.

Bible Text

James 2:18; Luke 7:36-50; John 3:1-15; John 4:1-26

Bible Background for Our Celebration

Experienced faith. The faith styles that Westerhoff names are evident in the people Jesus interacted with, from Pharisees to prostitutes. The first faith style is "experienced faith." In this style of faith, a person

learns by what he or she experiences. Moreover, in this style we want our experience to be consistent with what people say. In James 2:18b we are told, "Show me your faith apart from your works, and I by my works will show you my faith." Faith is not just belief. It is real life experience that puts what we believe into action.

Jesus says, "You shall love the Lord your God with all your heart, and with all your soul, and with all your strength, and with all your mind, and your neighbor as yourself" (Luke 10:27). For people with experienced faith, Jesus is the perfect example of saying and doing the same thing. He was consistent. He not only said we should love others, he modeled loving one another. He welcomed the sinners and outcasts and ate with them. He let them experience his love. People of experienced faith have little tolerance for hypocrisy. We find stories such as the Good Samaritan powerful because they are accounts of people putting faith into action and experience. We like it when Jesus allowed the children to come to him even when he was busy or tired or frustrated. The real life experience is in sync with what Jesus was saying all along—the powerless, the weak, and the innocent are important to God.

Affiliative faith. The second faith style is "affiliative faith." People need to know that they belong and that they can give to the life of the community. Throughout Jesus' ministry he empowered people by accepting them. They knew they belonged, even when society said they didn't. The disciples scoffed when the sinful woman anointed Jesus with her tears and perfume. They did not understand that the woman belonged and that her faith was great. Which one of us does not want to belong, to feel that we are part of the body of Christ?

Searching faith. Jesus did not give pat answers but allowed people to struggle with ideas. He taught through stories that pushed people to question assumptions and see new insights. People who come to faith in this way are said to have a "searching faith." Searching faith recognizes that doubt and critical thinking are a part of the journey. Jesus recognized that we need to reflect on what we believe and struggle with new insights. The Pharisee Nicodemus, who came to Jesus at night with questions of faith, represents this kind of faith in the Bible (John 3:1-15).

Owned faith. Only after people have searched for themselves and struggled with what they believe can they "own" their faith. Often when a person can claim faith and own it, he or she desires to put his or her faith into action. Jesus invited people through his interaction with them to own their faith. This style traditionally has been called conversion. When the Samaritan woman encountered Jesus, she asked questions and raised doubts. When she believed, she was transformed and had to tell others of the one "who told me everything I have ever done." A person who owns his or her faith will want to share it with others (John 4:1-26). When Zacchaeus the tax collector was hiding in a tree, Jesus noticed him and said that they would go and eat at his house that very day. Zacchaeus proclaimed that he was a changed man. He gave money to the poor and returned money to those whom he had cheated.

Faith Nugget

Jesus meets us where we are and invites us to expand our faith.

Early Preparation

Arrange for a woman to deliver the printed monologues. For the monologues, simple costume changes are required. For instance, a scarf worn in several positions could signify different characters.

Engage the youth group and/or younger youth in the dramatization of *The Giving Tree.*

Invite a soloist to sing verses of four hymns. Position him or her to one side of your gathering place. The soloist may sing *a cappella* or with simple accompaniment.

Arrange on stage a bare branch set in a bucket full of sand. If you have a larger congregation, you may need more branches in separate bunches. Cut tree leaves from construction paper, one for each person in the congregation. Punch a hole at the stem end. After the teaching, hand each person a leaf to write on. Later in the celebration, people will hang the leaves on the branches with paper clips. Be sure to have enough paper clips, one for each person.

Gather materials for putting together kits for relief projects.

You will need

❏ a worship leader
❏ an actor for monologues
❏ a scarf with fringe
❏ paper leaves with a paper clip attached to each one (enough leaves for each member of the congregation to have one)
❏ one or more bare branches set in buckets full of sand
❏ a soloist
❏ a copy of Shel Silverstein's *The Giving Tree*
❏ narrator and mimes for *The Giving Tree*
❏ activity leaders and supplies

Name of your church
The Many Ways of Faith
Celebrating Unity and Variety in Faith

Gathering Hymns

Call to Worship

Faith Styles in Story and Song

• A Young Mother's Monologue (Experienced Faith)
Solo ....“For God so loved us”
Experienced Faith Activity

• The Giving Tree (Belonging Faith)
Solo ....“God loves all his many people”
Belonging Faith Activity

• Nicodemus's Monologue (Searching Faith)
Solo .....“Open my eyes, that I may see”
Searching Faith Activity

• Zacchaeus's Monologue (Owned Faith)
Solo ....“I sought the Lord”
Owned Faith Activity

Hymn ....“Now thank we all our God”

Offering
    Prayer of Dedication and Blessing

Hymn ....“O God, your constant care”

Benediction

The Celebration

Gathering Music

As people gather, sing two or three hymns, such as "Here in this place," "Come let us all unite to sing," "Great is the Lord," "In thee is gladness," and "Obey my voice." Or allow people to suggest hymns that are important expressions of their faith.

Call to Worship

Leader: Every living thing needs the right environment to grow. A tree needs sunlight, the right soil, and rain. Each of us is a living creature and if we are to grow in our faith life, we also need the right environment. If our faith is to expand or grow into all that it can be, it also needs the right elements. Let us come together in this place at this time to be an environment. Let us be a rich soil of encouragement, a beacon of light helping others find the path, and a refreshing rain, giving living water to those who thirst.

Faith Styles in Story and Song

Leader: Faith is like a tree. With every year and every experience, it adds a layer of growth. We do not shed the old understanding of faith. It is at our core. We grow. We build on early learnings. We expand and change. But like the sapling that is every bit as much a tree as the giant oak, so is the faith of a five-year-old as authentic as that of the old sage.

Today we celebrate the rich variety of ways to be faithful. A series of monologues will show us the kind of faith that comes from experiencing Jesus' teachings in real life, the kind of faith that comes from knowing we are accepted, the kind of faith that we know by searching, and the kind of faith we know beyond all reason and can claim for ourselves. You may see your own faith in one or all of these stories. But no matter which kind of faith we have or how we got there,

we are the faithful, and we are richer for all our variety. Like the big oak, we are stronger for all our layers of growth.

Experienced Faith—A Young Mother's Monologue (Mark 10:13-16)

Find the script for this monologue in the resource section for this celebration. When the worship leader finishes, there is a slight pause and the "young mother" begins her monologue behind the group and makes her way to the front. The costume is a scarf draped on her head. A scarf with fringe can be used for another character. The worship leader sits during her presentation.

Solo: "For God so loved us" (see Resources for This Celebration).

Experienced Faith Activity

Emphasize that "experienced faith" knows the gospel message through real-life experience. What Jesus said and what Jesus did were the same. Living out our beliefs makes faith authentic. Send people to stations to put faith into action by assembling health kits, school kits, food boxes or other donations for relief projects in which your church participates. This would be a good time to make cards for a sister congregation in another community or country.

Belonging Faith—*The Giving Tree*, by Shel Silverstein

Mimes take their places. You will need a narrator, a young boy, and a young man to play the boy in later years. You will also need four people to play the tree. One person, dressed in brown, kneels on all fours. The other three, dressed in brown pants and green shirts, stand around the person who is kneeling, forming a circle. They are facing outward and position their arms at various heights to be the branches. The narrator and actors come forward. The people playing the tree take their position in the middle of the stage. The two people playing the boy stand off to the side with their backs to the audience. Off to one side a narrator tells the story into a microphone.

Solo: "God loves all his many people"
(see Resources for This Celebration)

Belonging Faith Activity

Take a group photo. Using a wide-angle lens on a 35mm camera or a disposable panoramic camera, take a picture of the whole congregation. If the group is very large, take the photo in sections from one position, and join the photos together when they are developed. Show that everyone belongs to the church.

Searching Faith—Nicodemus (John 3:1-15)

See the resources section of this celebration for a monologue script. The actor enters and stands with her back to the congregation. This time the scarf is draped across her shoulders like a prayer shawl. She turns around to give the reading.

Solo: "Open my eyes, that I may see"

Searching Faith Activity

A searching faith is one in which people find meaning as they wrestle with great questions and mysteries of Christian faith. Any question is fair. Create a graffiti wall. Prior to gathering for the celebration, cover one wall of the room with newsprint or butcher paper. Provide markers, paint, or drawing utensils. Ask people to quote Moses, Jeremiah, Nathaniel, or others in the Bible who had questions, who searched for answers. In addition, have people write on the wall the searching questions they have pondered in their own faith journeys.

Owned Faith—Zacchaeus (Luke 19:1-10)

When people are settled again, the actor/reader turns again toward the congregation and presents the monologue. This time she wears the scarf as a sash or turban.

Solo: "I sought the Lord" (see Resources for This Celebration)

After the solo the soloist and the actor exit together.

Owned Faith Activity

Owned faith is characterized by conversion. Encourage people to tell their personal stories of conversion. Set up four to eight storytelling stations. Post one person with a story of conversion at each station. Allow the congregation to move from one station to another, hearing several stories. Look for storytellers who have widely different stories of faith—a lightening bolt experience like Paul's conversion from fear to courage for the sake of the Gospel, a conversion from wealth to simplicity, a change from master to servant, or other types of faith conversions. Consider including the stories of children or people who can tell about conversion at a very young age.

Hymn

When all have returned to their seats, ask those who are able to stand if they can identify with the woman and child, then the boy and the tree, then Nicodemus, then Zacchaeus. Hopefully, all will be standing as one body. Then sing "Now thank we all our God" or other thanksgiving hymn.

Offering

Leader: Let us give thanks for all the people who as teachers have touched our lives. We are passing out paper leaves. I invite you to write a person's name on the leaf who has blessed your faith life. Then come forward and put the leaves on the trees. Bring your monetary gifts as well. Take a moment to reflect and write something on your leaf.

As people hang leaves on the trees, sing celebrative songs, such as "Seek ye first the kingdom of God," "This little light of mine," and "Will you let me be your servant."

Prayer of Dedication and Blessing

Thank you God for being with us and being a constant in our lives. Thank you for the many wonderful people you have brought into our lives. They have touched us deeply, enabling us to grow and expand in our faith. For them we will be ever grateful.

In this community of believers and beyond, help us to provide an environment where others can grow and learn about you. We each are unique and have much to offer. Bless each of us, wherever we are in our faith journey. Help us to continue to expand in our faith life. Bless our offering of money to the good of your kingdom. Amen.

Hymn

Sing a hymn of faith, such as "O God, your constant care."

Benediction

One: Keep the Lord's commands in your hearts.
Let love and faithfulness never leave you;
bind them around your neck,
write them on the tablet of your heart.

All: We will trust the Lord with all our hearts,
and lean not on our own understanding;
in all our ways we will acknowledge the Lord,
and the Lord will make our paths straight.

— based on Proverbs 3:1b, 3, 5-6

Resources for This Celebration

Monologues

Experienced Faith—A Young Mother's Monologue (Mark 10:13-16)

"Don't bother him. He doesn't have time for you. He has a great many things on his mind." That is what the men around Jesus said to me when I brought my child to him.

My name is Sarah. I was just a young mother when I first heard about Jesus. A friend of mine had heard Jesus teach. She saw him heal a great many people. She came back so excited that I decided to investigate for myself. When I saw and heard Jesus, I knew that he was indeed a great Teacher. I decided to bring my three-year-old child for him to touch. I wanted the best for my little boy. I knew his touch would be a blessing. Some other parents had the same idea. When we got close, those words are what we heard from the disciples. One said that Jesus did not have time for us. Another said that we should not bother the Master who had a great many things on his mind. Jesus heard them and said in a loud voice, "Let the children come to me, and do not hinder them." He reached out his arms and the children came to him. He lifted one child and held her in his lap and blessed her. He also said, "Anyone who will not receive the kingdom of God like a child will never enter it." That got the disciples' attention. The way Jesus acted was like he had all the time in the world for these little ones. My little boy tends to be shy, but Jesus did not push him. He allowed my son slowly to become familiar with him. Before I knew it, little Aaron was up on his lap, receiving a blessing. It brought tears to my eyes. Aaron was all smiles when we left. He could not stop talking about Jesus. He knew he was special in Jesus' eyes. He was loved.

Searching Faith—Nicodemus (John 3:1-15)

I was so confused. I had gone to hear Jesus, this man who was causing such an uproar, preach. Thoughts about what he said and did kept circling in my mind. Around and around they went, finding no place to rest. As a Pharisee I hold to the strict obedience of the law. In this way we are preparing ourselves for the coming of the Messiah. I am devoted to living by the covenant down to the last detail.

Yet, as I listened to Jesus teach, I felt the foundation of my world-view being shaken. He teaches by telling stories. He never gives simple answers. He truly wanted us to struggle with the answers for ourselves. That impressed me. If he would have claimed he was God, I could have dismissed him as a blasphemer. Instead, my mind kept returning to the stories. The problem was that the answers I was coming up with did not fit into my usual way of thinking. I believe God places a great many demands on us and judges us in the end. But Jesus represents God as gracious and compassionate. Jesus warmly embraced the uneducated and notorious sinners. We have been separating ourselves from them. We earnestly seek God. Yet, I felt Jesus was trying to widen our perception of God, reaching beyond the traditional understanding that we hold. Other Pharisees oppose Jesus violently, so I could not ask them my questions about Jesus. They think he may endanger our precarious relationship with the Romans and damage our temple worship. I decided I needed to talk with him myself. So I came to Jesus at night hoping no one would see me.

My encounter with him left me more confused than ever. When I went to see him, all I knew for sure was that I did believe he was a teacher from God. I acknowledged that to him and he was off and running, teaching me by saying, "No one can see the kingdom of God unless he is born again." I was in the dust, trying to catch up. How can a person enter his mother's womb again? How could that be a possibility? Then he said, "I tell you the truth, no one can enter the kingdom of God unless he is born of water and the Spirit."

It surprised Jesus that I did not understand what he meant—"You must be born again." It was true that it was not a completely new idea to me. You see, when a person converts to Judaism, they are seen as being born again. Yet I struggled to make sense out of it all. He tried to help me by giving the example of the wind. We hear its sound but do not know where it comes from or where it is going. It is the same way with everyone born of the Spirit. Still, I felt like I was wading through mud. I asked, "How can this be?"

As you can imagine, I left with more questions than answers. Nothing that Jesus said is easy for me to understand. One answer just leads to more questions. But I know in my heart, there is something special about Jesus.

Owned Faith—Zacchaeus (Luke 19:1-10)

Jericho is a wonderful town. There is so much beauty around. There is a great palm forest, a balsam grove that sends out a scent for miles, and gardens of roses. More importantly, Jericho is in a key location in the Jordan valley. It produces great tax revenues! You probably know that I acquired a lot of wealth as a tax collector. You would think that I would be happy in such a beautiful place. I am not. People put me in the same category as murderers and robbers. They barred one from the synagogue. You know how that makes a person feel? Lonely, very lonely. I do not belong anywhere. Then I heard about this Jesus. It is said that he welcomed tax collectors and sinners. I just had to see him. I heard he was coming by. It was dangerous for me to go out among people, but I didn't care anymore. I just wanted to see Jesus. Maybe, just maybe he would welcome me too.

All along the road, people were being mean to me. When I got closer to where the crowd was surrounding Jesus, people started making sure I could not see. As you can tell, I am not a very big man, so it is not very hard. I was scared I would never be able to see Jesus this way. So I decided to get out of the crowd. This gave me space to run ahead of the crowd to a large sycamore tree. I heaved myself up into the tree. It was difficult but I made it. From there I could see Jesus in the center of the crowd. Oh, it was perfect, he was actually going to be walking right under the tree. Suddenly, he stopped. He was looking up and talking to me. For a second, I did not hear what he said. Then I realized he was talking to me. He said, "Zacchaeus, come down immediately. I must stay at your house today." I came down quickly and gladly welcomed him. It was so wonderful to actually have someone want to be with me. I started to hear people mutter around us, "He has gone to be the guest of a sinner." Inside I knew that I had changed. The encounter with Jesus affected me deeply. I was not an outcast with Jesus. I said to the Lord, "Look, Lord! I'm giving half of my possessions to the poor, and if I have cheated anybody out of anything, I will pay back four times the amount." I am a changed man and it feels wonderful.

For God so loved us

GOTT IST DIE LIEBE 10 9 with refrain

1 For God so loved us, he sent the Sav - ior. For God so
2 He sent the Sav - ior, the bless'd Re - deem - er. He sent the
3 He bade me wel - come; oh word of mer - cy! He bade me
4 Glo - ry and hon - or, O Love e - ter - nal, to thee be

loved us, and loves me too.
Sav - ior to set me free.
wel - come; oh voice di - vine!
giv - en while life shall last.

Refrain

Love so un - end - ing,

I'll sing thy prais - es. God loves his chil - dren, loves e - ven me.

Text: August Rische, *Gott ist die Liebe;* tr. Esther C. Bergen (Sts. 1-3), *The Youth Hymnary,* © 1956, Faith & Life Press.
          Used by permission.
              The Hymn Book (St. 4 and refrain), 1960
              Translation (St. 4 and refrain) copyright © 1960 *The Hymn Book.* Used by permission of Kindred Productions.
Music: Thüringer melody, ca. 1840

God loves all his many people

85. 85 with refrain

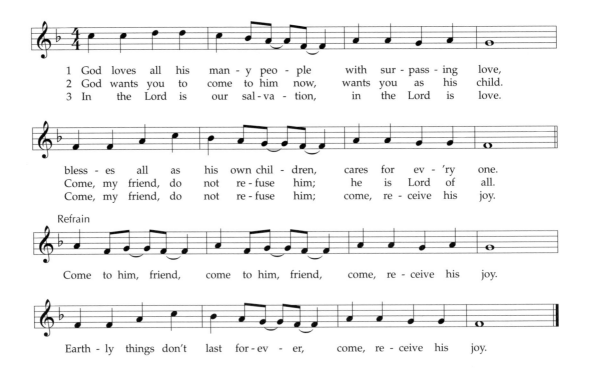

1 God loves all his man-y peo-ple   with sur-pass-ing love,
2 God wants you to come to him now,   wants you as his child.
3 In the Lord is our sal-va-tion,   in the Lord is love.

bless-es all as his own chil-dren,   cares for ev-'ry one.
Come, my friend, do not re-fuse him;   he is Lord of all.
Come, my friend, do not re-fuse him;   come, re-ceive his joy.

Refrain

Come to him, friend, come to him, friend,   come, re-ceive his joy.

Earth-ly things don't last for-ev-er,   come, re-ceive his joy.

Text: Lubunda Mukungu; tr. revised by Anna Junke, *International Songbook*, Mennonite World Conference, 1978, alt.
         Translation copyright © 1978, 1990 Mennonite World Conference, Strasbourg, France. Used by permission.
Music: Tshiluba melody (Zaire), *International Songbook*, Mennonite World Conference, 1978

I sought the Lord

FAITH 10 10. 10 6

1 I sought the Lord, and af-ter-ward I knew he moved my
2 Thou didst reach forth thy hand and mine en-fold, I walked and
3 I find, I walk, I love, but, oh, the whole of love is

soul to seek him, seek-ing me. It was not I that
sank not on the storm-vexed sea. 'Twas not so much that
but my an-swer, Lord, to thee! For thou wert long be-

found, O Sav-ior true, no, I was found of thee.
I on thee took hold as thou, dear Lord, on me.
fore-hand with my soul, al-ways thou lov-edst me.

Text: *Holy Songs, Carols, and Sacred Ballads*, 1880
Music: J. Harold Moyer, 1965, *The Mennonite Hymnal*, 1969

Working in the Garden

Celebrating Creation

Compassion is the basis of all morality.
—*Arthur Schopenhauer*

Too often we have not understood our interdependence with nature. We have interpreted our role of having dominion over the earth and subduing it (Gen. 1:28) as meaning we can use the earth and its resources to our heart's content. We now realize that unless we become God's stewards ("The Lord God took the man and put him in the garden of Eden to till it and keep it" Gen. 2:15), we will have nothing to care for on this planet.

This celebration seeks to increase our compassion for God's wondrous creation. First, we will take time simply to notice the world around us and let ourselves be filled with awe at the wonder of it all. If we are able to recognize beauty, we can also feel the pain that comes when beauty is destroyed. We will listen to the cries of creation. If we hear the cries of a distressed earth, perhaps we can find creative ways to make amends—to seek justice for nature. Moreover, we may find that our spirituality is deepened when we have compassion for all that is around us.

Bible Text

Genesis 2:15; Leviticus 25:23-24; Hosea 2:18-21; Romans 8:18-27.

Bible Background for Our Celebration

In Genesis 2, God assigns human creatures the role of caretaker over the rest of creation. But after the fall, the corruption of human nature leads to greediness and a tendency to forget whose the world really is. In Leviticus 25:23-24, God says, "The land is mine; with me you are but aliens and tenants." But we have violated the earth in order to have a more comfortable living. When we look around and truly see the damage that has been done, we begin to feel the pain of our actions. Out of our suffering comes compassion and a desire to change our attitudes and actions.

The scripture states that creation will one day be liberated: "The creation itself will be set free from its bondage to decay and will obtain the freedom of the glory of the children of God" (Rom. 8:21). Likewise, in Hosea God describes the beautiful results when his covenant with Israel is renewed, "I will make for you a covenant on that day with

the wild animals, the birds of the air, and the creeping things of the ground; and I will abolish the bow, the sword, and war from the land; and I will make you lie down in safety."

With God's help and a renewed sense of responsibility for the stewardship of creation, we can work to change our ways. When this happens we will be able to celebrate God's wondrous creation and our acts of justice to preserve this great gift.

Faith Nugget

We celebrate God's great gift of creation and covenant with God to be humble caretakers of all God has given us.

Early Preparation

Review the entire celebration and begin to contact people to carry out tasks.

Assign someone to bring in items for the confession time and people to bring these items forward during the celebration. To perfect the timing, practice with those people who will be presenting them. Make copies of the "Litany of Confession" (in Resources for This Celebration) to hand out to the congregation.

Decide ahead of time whether you will hold this celebration outdoors. If so, you may want to conclude with a picnic.

You will need

❏ a storyteller
❏ a worship leader
❏ a song leader
❏ a copy of "The Creation," by James Weldon Johnson
❏ a dancer
❏ Wonder Center leaders and materials
❏ copies of the "Litany of Confession"
❏ large sheets of paper and markers

Name of your church
Working in the Garden
Celebrating Creation

Gathering Hymns......................"Sing praise
to God who reigns"
"For the beauty of the earth"

Opening Prayer

"The Creation" ..... James Weldon Johnson

Creation Hymns

Wonder Centers
1. Wonder About the Sun
2. Wonder About Nocturnal Animals
3. Wonder About Water and Water
Creatures
4. Wonder About Land and Plant Life
5. Wonder About Animals, Birds, and
Humans
6. Wonder About the Sabbath

Gather Again

Hymn ...."This is the day the
Lord has made"

Litany of Confession

Working Toward Justice

Offering............................"O healing river"
"New earth, heavens new"

Prayer of Dedication

Sending............"You shall go out with joy"

The Celebration

Gathering Hymns

Sing hymns that praise God for the wonders of creation, such as "Sing praise to God who reigns" and "For the beauty of the earth."

Opening Prayer

Leader: Creator God, you have set the world in motion. The beauty you have created and are creating still is all around us. Open our hearts and minds to the splendor that you splash on the landscapes outside our doors. May we see with new eyes the wondrous things you have created. Amen.

A Reading: "The Creation"

As someone recites James Weldon Johnson's "The Creation," someone else interprets the poem through dance. The poem will be most effective if recited slowly and dramatically. Encourage the reader to listen to a professional recording of this poem, available in most public libraries.

Hymns

Sing two more creation hymns, such as "God of the earth, the sky, the sea," "All things bright and beautiful," and "This is the day the Lord has made."

Wonder Centers

Dismiss the group to visit the Wonder Centers in fifteen-minute intervals. Ring a bell every fifteen minutes to indicate it is time to move to another center. Each person will have time to go to three or four centers.

1. Wonder About the Sun. There are three activities in this center. Begin by having everyone stand in the sunshine if weather permits. Have participants close their eyes and lift their faces to the sun. Ask them what it feels like. Note that even though the sun is ninety-three mil-lion miles from the earth, we can feel its heat on our faces. How amazing!

a. Make a rainbow. You will need prisms, a garden hose, and an outdoor faucet. Although we usually think of sunlight as colorless, the rainbow shows us the full array of colors in sunlight: red, orange, yellow, blue, green, indigo, and violet. Rainbows are made by drops of water acting like a prism, breaking up the sunlight into its colors. Find a glass prism, a flashlight, and a white piece of paper. Stand the prism up on the paper. Take the flashlight and shine it through the prism. Adjust the paper under the prism so that the light passing through will fall on the paper. Notice how the white light breaks up into a rainbow of colors as it passes through the prism.

If a garden hose is available, turn the nozzle to a fine, misty spray. Have one participant stand with his or her back to the sun, holding the hose high. Instruct the others to look into the spray. They will see the many different colors of the rainbow. Ask people to name the colors they see.

b. Make a sun reflector. You will need construction paper or scrap cardboard, scissors, aluminum foil, glue, string, and hole punch. Make different patterns out of construction paper or scrap cardboard. Glue bits of aluminum foil on them and press them very flat. Somewhere on the shape, write "Let there be light" (Gen. 1:3). Punch a hole at the top of each reflector and attach a piece of string for hanging near a window. See how the light sparkles when you hold up the reflector.

c. Marvel at the sun's energy. The heat from the sun makes the wind blow. The air covering the earth is warmer at the equator than at the poles because the equator is closer to the sun. As the air near the equator is warmed, it rises into the atmosphere and moves toward the North and South Poles where it cools.

Warmer air coming in behind it pushes the cooler air back to the equator, and the cycle starts all over again. The moving air is what we call wind. We can't see wind. We can only see what it does. For instance, wind makes a windmill go around or leaves flutter through the air.

Make a pinwheel to demonstrate how the sun works to give us wind energy. Give everyone an unsharpened pencil with an eraser on the end and a perfect square of paper (9" x 9"). Use a ruler to draw a diagonal line from one corner to the opposite corner of the paper. Repeat with the other two corners. There should be a large X on the paper. The place where the two diagonals cross is the exact center of the square.

Each corner of the paper is now divided in two, making eight corners altogether. Number each corner, beginning with the top left and going clockwise. Cut along each diagonal to within ½ inch of the center. Take corners 1, 3, 5, and 7, and pull them towards the center of the square. Put a thumbtack through all layers and through the center of the paper. Then push the tack through the eraser of the pencil, but not too tightly or the pinwheel won't turn. Blow gently on the corners of the pinwheel. As the blades of the pinwheel catch the air, the pinwheel will turn.

2. Wonder About Nocturnal Animals. God created some animals to be active at night instead of in the day. These animals live and hunt in the dark. They must rely on other senses besides vision to move about, to hunt, and to find their mates. As a way to appreciate these animals and God's creativity, we will pretend to be common nocturnal animals.

A bat navigates by sending out sound waves. These waves then bounce off objects around them. By listening for the wave to return to their ears, bats can tell the size of an object and how far away it is. This is called echolocation. Simulate echolocation by playing a modified version of the child's game "Marco Polo." Blindfold one person (the bat) who will send out the signal "beep." In response, the other players say "beep." The blindfolded person tries to tag someone in the room by listening to the echoing beeps.

If the bat catches someone, that bat takes his or her place.

Fireflies cannot hear or smell so their sense of sight is highly important to them. To locate a mate, the male sends out flashes of light. He watches for a signal to be returned by a female. This is a challenge, for in a given area there might be numerous species of fireflies, each having a different signal. We will simulate this experience by playing the firefly game. If the group is large, play the game with ten people at a time—you will need an even number. Give each participant a piece of paper on which a signal pattern has been written. Give the same pattern to two people. One long flash followed by two short flashes or one short flash is an example of a signal pattern. Give everyone a flashlight and darken the room. Have partners locate one another by finding the matching signal.

3. Wonder About Water and Water Creatures. Begin by having the group imitate the sounds of a thunderstorm. Flickering lights resemble lightening. Drumming heels on the floor sound like thunder. Rubbing palms together, softly at first and then harder and more rapidly, imitates the sound of rain. Drumming hands on knees sounds like a real downpour. Try each of these.

a. Water is an amazing substance. Ask if anyone knows what percentage of our bodies is made up of water. Ask if anyone knows how much of the earth's surface is made up of water. Seventy-five percent is the answer to both questions. Clearly, clean water is very important for each human being and the planet Earth.

Divide into two groups. Have one group draw the outline of a human being on a large sheet of poster paper, and on another sheet of poster paper, have the other group draw the outline of the planet Earth. On the posters have each group make a list of "ingredients" in order of quantity, like the list you would see on the label of a cereal box (from most to least): Human being—water, bones, muscle, body organs, skin; Earth's surface—water, rocks, iron, soil. Then compare the ingredients. Note how vital it is for human beings and the planet Earth to have clean water. Ask what happens when the water is polluted. Make up slogans about good health requiring clean water, and put them on each poster.

b. Learn about whales. God made many wondrous creatures. The whale is similar to a human being in a number of ways. See if the group can name them. For example, both are mammals that breathe air and feed their young milk produced by the mother.

Whales are also very different from people. Whales' eyes are on the sides of their heads. That means that they can see in almost every direction, except for one blind spot. Have everyone hold three or four fingers of one hand between their eyes and over their nose. Now have them use their other hand to wave something in front of their face. Is there a place they cannot see? Neither can the whale. They cannot see directly in front.

A whale breathes through its blow hole, which is used for breathing only, not for smelling. A whale's blowhole does not have a sense of smell like our nose does. Where is a whale's blowhole? Have participants place a finger on their noses and move it from their nose, over their head, until they reach the back of their neck. That is where a whale's nose would be. Unlike human beings, whales can hold their breath for thirty minutes or more. Have everyone hold their breath while you time them. See who can hold their breath the longest.

Whales have small holes right behind their eyes. These are their ears. Whales have very keen hearing that allows them to navigate through murky or dark water by using echolocation. By making special sounds and listening to the echoes, they can tell how far away something is and how big it is. Choose a person to be "It" and blindfold him. Then scatter the rest of the group around the room and instruct them to stay where they are planted. When everyone is in place, choose someone to be a counterpart to It. It will try to make his way to the counterpart, navigating by sound. As It calls out "whale!" every few seconds, the counterpart will respond "Whale!" to guide him. All the others in the room call out "here!" repeatedly so that It can avoid running into them while making

his way to his counterpart. When the counterparts find each other, choose a new It and counterpart and start again.

Have participants hold out their hands in front of them. Point out that whales have flippers on the sides of their bodies that help them steer as they swim. The flippers have five "fingers" like people do. Have participants bend their arms at their sides and flip their "flippers" as they imagine themselves being whales twisting and turning in the water.

c. Most animals don't have fingers and arms, so if they become entangled in debris, they have a hard time freeing themselves. Have participants imagine themselves as baby seals or water fowl playing around when suddenly their head accidentally goes through a set of plastic six-pack rings that picnickers have thrown into the water. To help participants realize how difficult it would be for the animal to free itself, have each person hold out their hand. Loop a rubber band around each person's thumb and stretch it over the back side of the hand (not the palm) and loop it around the little finger. Do not try to remove the rubber band until everyone is "entangled" in this piece of "litter." Now, without using the other hand or any body part, try to get the rubber band off. It is almost impossible. Baby seals and water fowl entangled in this kind of debris will grow until the ring is so tight it chokes them. This is one reason we need to keep our oceans, lakes, and rivers free of litter so that God's creatures will be safe.

d. Make a picture of the journey of water. Water makes an incredible journey from the sky to land to sky again. Have the group create a mural showing the water cycle described here.

The water cycle begins in a cloud. From the cloud a snowflake falls onto a mountain. When it stays cold on the mountain, the water stays frozen. Then as spring comes, the snow beings to melt and moves down the mountainside. The water comes together to form a stream that rushes down the mountainside. Numerous streams meet and run into the river at different points. The river continues down until it meets the ocean. Rivers join the ocean at numerous places. There the sun warms the water and it becomes water vapor. The water vapor rises into the air to make clouds and the cycle begins again.

e. Find out who lives in the water. Have the group list as many creatures as they can that live in a body of water. The list might include turtles, toads, snails, crayfish, small fish, insects, larger fish, birds, geese, and ducks. Ocean life includes whales, shrimp, dolphins, mussels, clams, jellyfish, scallops, and crabs. Give everyone a sponge and have them cut out the shape of their favorite creature.

4. Wonder About Land and Plant Life.
Open by reading *The Lorax* by Dr. Seuss. Borrow the book from a public library or a member of the congregation.

a. Visit the earth's rain forests. On a globe or map, show where rain forests are located. To help younger children, show where you are located and other familiar points of interest; then show the rain forests. Talk about how trees from the rain forest are used to make many different items. Identify items in the room that are made of wood.

Many spices also come from rain forests. Bring in different spices, such as allspice, cardamom, cloves, cinnamon, ginger, mace, nutmeg, chili powder, black pepper, paprika, and vanilla. Have participants sniff the different spices and try to name them. Hand out Red Hots candies to eat as a reminder of the importance of rain forests.

b. All living things depend on soil, directly or indirectly, as a source of food. To demonstrate how little of the earth's surface is actually used for food production, cut up an apple in the following manner.

• Cut the apple into four equal parts. Three parts represent the oceans of the world. The fourth part represents the land area.

• Cut the land section in half lengthwise. Now you have two one-eighth pieces. One section represents land such as deserts, swamps, Antarctic, Arctic, and mountain regions. The other one-eighth section represents land where man can live and grow food.

• Slice this one-eighth section crosswise into four equal parts. Three of these one thirty-second sections represent the areas of the world that have been developed by man or are too rocky, too wet, too hot, or too poor for production.

• Carefully peel the last one thirty-second section. This small bit of peeling represents the soil of our earth on which mankind depends for food production!

c. Make a seed viewer. Give each person a clear plastic cup, and have them line the inside walls of the cup with construction paper. Fill the cup with a wadded-up paper towel. Give each person two bean seeds to place between the plastic cup and the construction paper. Then wet the towel thoroughly until the construction paper is moist. Each person can take his or her seed viewer home and place it in a warm spot. They should add water each day and watch the seeds grow.

d. Collect seeds. If you are in or near a wooded area or field, give each person an old nylon stocking or tube sock filled with crumpled newspaper and tied shut with a long string. To collect the seeds, drag your collector (stuffed sock) across a forest floor or through a field. Then examine the socks with a magnifying lens, if possible. Have people talk about what they see, especially noting the variety of seeds. Recycle the newspaper after this activity.

e. Do leaf rubbings. Collect a variety of leaves, being careful not to damage trees or plants. Arrange them face down on a table. Put a piece of drawing paper over the arrangement of leaves. Use the side of a wax crayon to rub lightly and evenly over the paper. Leaves with pronounced veins work best. Talk about the role the leaves play for trees. The green hue in a leaf is from chlorophyll, which uses the sunlight to combine water and air. The resulting sugars and starches feed the plant. When the leaves turn colors they are no longer making food for the tree.

5. Wonder About Animals, Birds, and Humans.

a. As a way to appreciate each animal and realize that more and more are becoming extinct through poaching or loss of habitat, we will play musical chairs with a twist. Make a circle of chairs with one chair for each person. Put a picture of a dinosaur on the back of one chair. This is the "chair of extinction." Have each participant represent a different animal, but limit the animals to several groups or species, such as water animals, large jungle animals, etc. Begin like musical chairs, with the music playing while the group walks around the outside of the circle. When the music stops, everyone sits down in a chair. Whoever sits in the "chair of extinction" is out. Remove one of the chairs and continue playing. When one or two species have become extinct, stop the game and talk about how it felt to watch their own or another species become extinct.

b. Make dried fruit garland bird feeders. Some birds love dried fruit. Provide a variety of dried figs, apricots, apples, fresh cranberries, and toasted oat cereal for this activity. Using large, blunt needles with large eyes, thread dental floss through the needle and use it to string the dried fruit into a garland. The younger children will need assistance. Send the finished garlands home in plastic food storage bags. Suggest that the garlands be draped on trees where people can observe the birds that come to the garland to eat.

c. Hunt for insects and animals. Divide into pairs and go for a short hike (urban, suburban, or rural). Pair very young children who cannot write with older children or adults. Have pairs keep track of all the animals, birds, and insects they notice. Set a time limit and gather again to compare lists.

6. Wonder About the Sabbath. Provide meditative music and a scripture text printed on paper that has space for journaling below the text. Also hand out hymnals. This Wonder Center provides time to express appreciation to God for the sabbath. It is a time to renew our focus on God and renew our strength. According to the original Hebrew in Exodus 31:17, "On the seventh day God rested and let out a sigh." In the environment there is naturally both activity and rest. The same is true for humans. At times we are active and at times we need rest. If we are continually working and never resting, our physical, emotional, spiritual selves are unbalanced. If we do not take time to praise God and listen to what God is trying to tell us, our spiritual selves become off-center.

Play relaxing music as people enter. Give each person a piece of paper with the scripture text of Matthew 6:25-34, which talks about how God will care for us. Participants read the text silently a number of times and reflect on what God is saying. Allow about half of the allotted time for reflection. Then give time for those who wish to share their thoughts. The group also may want to talk about how they observed the sabbath as children and how they observe it now. Finally, worship together by singing favorite hymns as people suggest them.

Gather Again

Ring the bell for the last time. Direct people back to the gathering place and begin singing a favorite hymn of creation until all are gathered.

Hymn

When everyone has returned, sing "This is the day the Lord has made." Try singing this song antiphonally in two groups. Group 1 sings the first phrase. Group 2 repeats it. Group 1 sings the next phrase. Group 2 repeats it, and so on. When the words repeat on the last chorus, the congregation sings in unison.

Litany of Confession

Bring the confession symbols, gathered ahead of time, to the celebration worship center while the group reads the confession responsively. It is not necessary to coordinate the presentation of the item with its mention in the confession. Simply bring the items to a table and group them into a "still life," a focal point for the celebration. Items include plastic six-pack pop can rings, a balloon, aluminum cans, a jug of water, a foam cup or plate, a newspaper, a statue or picture of an endangered specie, a plastic bottle, a quart of motor oil, cinnamon. Add others that you think of. Find the "Litany of Confession" in Resources for This Celebration.

Working Toward Justice

Following the confession, divide into groups of four or five people (not larger). Give each group a different topic from the litany. Ask them to think of ways they can make a difference. These should be ideas that can be implemented realistically. Give each group a large piece of paper and a marker to write down ideas. Sheets will be collected during the offering. After the celebration, post the sheets where everyone can look at them in the weeks ahead. Publish the results in the church newsletter.

Offering

As a way of making a commitment to caring for God's creation, have the groups bring their commitment lists to the center of the celebration and place them on top of the items of confession. See this as an offering. Pass the offering plates as groups are taking their lists to the center. As the offering is collected, sing "O healing river," "New earth, heavens new," or another hymn of renewal.

Prayer of Dedication

All: Penetrate our hardened hearts with your mercy, O God.
Ignite a passion within us to care for your earth.
Instill in us love for all of creation.
Guide us to live lightly on your wondrous planet. Amen.

Sending

Sing "You shall go out with joy" or another song of joy and celebration. This one can be sung over and over as the congregation processes out.

Resources for This Celebration

Litany of Confession

All: We celebrate the beauty around us,
the sun, moon, and stars,
the land and seas,
the trees and plant life,
the insects, birds, and animals.

One: We confess we do not always use the resources on this wondrous planet wisely. Hear our words of confession.

All: I was driving my car two blocks to a friend's house when I heard the air say,

One: "See all the pollutants that go into the air; please don't drive when it's not necessary."

All: I threw out plastic six-pack rings without snipping them when I heard a seal say,

One: "A hundred thousand mammals are caught each year in plastic rings."

All: I let a helium balloon go at a celebration and watched it float away when I heard a turtle say,

One: "When animals eat broken or deflated balloons that fall to the ground, they suffer from blockages that eventually starve them."

All: I was in a hurry and did not see a recycling box for aluminum cans when I heard the land say,

One: "Aluminum cans can be recycled again and again instead of lying in a landfill."

All: I was brushing my teeth and letting the water run when I heard the water say,

One: "Just by turning off the water while you brush your teeth, you can save enough water to fill a swimming pool each year."

All: I did not bring a mug to work, so I reached for a plastic foam cup when I heard the earth say,

One: "Enough foam cups are used every year to circle me 436 times."

All: I read a newspaper and threw it in the wastebasket when I heard a tree say,

One: "Five hundred thousand trees could be saved each day if everyone would recycle the forty-five million newspapers read each day."

All: I saw a beautiful piece of ivory jewelry and wanted to buy it when I heard an African elephant say,

One: "Half of all my brothers and sisters have been killed in the last ten years for the ivory in our tusks. Every week, nearly twenty types of plants and animals become extinct."

All: I reached to buy orange juice in a plastic bottle when I heard the earth say,

One: "Every hour, Americans use 2.5 million plastic bottles and most of them are thrown away."

All: I was changing my oil and allowing the old oil to spill onto the ground when I heard the groundwater say,

One: "A quart of motor oil that seeps into the ground can pollute 250,000 gallons of drinking water."

All: I was cold and turned up the thermostat when I heard the fossil fuels say,

One: "Five hundred thousand barrels of oil would be saved every day, if everyone would turn down the thermostat six degrees and put on a sweater instead."

All: I was looking at some furniture made of mahogany when I heard a rain forest say,

One: "In one minute, one hundred acres of rain forests are cut down; that is enough to cover fifty football fields. More than half of the world's plants and animals live in rain forests."

All: Forgive us God, when we have failed to hear the pain of your creation around us. Forgive us God, when we have used the earth's resources wastefully. Help us to seek justice for your creation. Amen.

Walking in the Light

Celebrating Missions

> Happy are they who know that discipleship simply means the life which springs from grace, and that grace simply means discipleship.
> —*Dietrich Bonhoeffer*

As the moon reflects the light of the sun to the world at night, so we are called to reflect Christ's light in a world of spiritual darkness. The moon is not the source of the light, nor are we the source of our own light. To be able to provide light, we must walk in the light ourselves, living according to God's will.

This celebration calls us to focus on the joyful purpose Christ gave his followers: to be the light for the world. We want to celebrate all that we are doing as a body of believers to provide that light to our communities and our world. As we follow the will of God in our hearts as well as in our actions, we shine forth as the noonday sun.

Bible Text

Isaiah 58:1-10; Matthew 25:31-46; John 1:4-5; 8:12

Bible Background for Our Celebration

In Isaiah 58, the prophet, God's representative, calls the people to account. The people wonder why God doesn't answer their prayers even though they fast with sackcloth and ashes. The prophet tells them what a true fast involves. Is it not "to loose the bonds of injustice, to undo the thongs of the yoke, to let the oppressed go free, and to break every yoke? Is it not to share your bread with the hungry, and to bring the homeless poor into your house; when you see the naked, to cover them, and not to hide yourself from your own kin?" Light and healing will be the reward for pleasing God in this way.

Jesus is described, especially in John's Gospel, as the light shining in the darkness. He describes himself by saying "I am the light of the world. Whoever follows me will never walk in darkness, but will have the light of life" (John 8:12). In Ephesians the Christians are also described as children of the light. And being children of the light carries a responsibility; it involves living a certain way. Lives lived in the light will bear the fruits of the light, such as goodness, righteousness, and truth (Eph. 5:9). The light will aid us in discerning what is pleasing to the Lord. We are called to expose the deeds of darkness and, in this way, bring healing to our world.

Jesus' parable in Matthew 25:31-46 tells us that God's judgment will correspond to how we respond

to human need. We are called to respond with a loving heart and not a calculating mind. Jesus tells us to feed the hungry person, give the thirsty person a drink, welcome the stranger, clothe the naked, cheer the sick, and visit the prisoner. When we help the least of these, we are living as children of the light.

Faith Nugget

We are to reflect God's light in the world. To do so we must strive to meet the needs of those around us.

Early Preparation

This celebration calls for personal contact with a missionary either by speaker phone, if possible, or by letter. If you are working with missionaries in a foreign land, allow plenty of time for international mail and international telephone systems. But don't forget about the people in your church who do mission work near home. In either case, arrange in advance to have missionaries or volunteers who are supported by your congregation prepare a letter or a talk for the congregation. Suggest that they tell how their work is going. Also, in the spirit of the New Testament Epistles, ask the missionaries to include words of encouragement for the gathered group. If you choose to talk directly with the mission workers, arrange to do so during the service by planning with them in advance so they will be by the phone. Set up a speaker phone by a microphone so everyone can hear the conversation. In response, your congregation may wish to sing a song for the missionary to hear over the phone.

At least one month to six weeks in advance, ask someone to take slide pictures or prepare a video of people in the congregation in their everyday work or school or home setting, especially work that helps others. Create a sign-up sheet for those who are willing to have their picture taken. Ask for the address of their work place, school, or home and an appropriate time for the photos to be taken. Allow a second week for the sign-up in case people must get permission from their employer or teacher to have a guest.

Prepare a video or slide show presentation of people at work. Use a song or medley of songs such as "We Are the Light of the World" from Godspell, and "Here Am I, Send Me," by Keith Green, or other songs of discipleship.

Invite representatives from the mission board or a local mission to give presentations during activity time.

Ask someone to tell the story found in Resources for This Celebration: "The Candlemaker's Contest." Give the storyteller plenty of notice so he or she can practice the story with candles.

Put together a pop bottle band several weeks in advance. Using water, tune the pop bottles to the eight notes of the major scale or twelve notes, including half steps. The more water, the higher the note. It is best to check the pitch with a piano. Pour water in small increments. Label each bottle with the note it represents and mark the level of water for future reference. Each time you use the bottles, you will need to tune them again by adjusting the water levels. Each player gets one bottle (two if very coordinated) and one flashlight. The band will be playing in a darkened room. When the player sounds the note by blowing across the top of the bottle, he or she turns on the flashlight and holds it to the bottom of the bottle. For added effect, put a drop of food coloring in each bottle. The light will shine on the colored water and on the face of the player, creating a fun visual effect.

Assign a small group leader to read a book about mission, such as *Witness: Empowering the Church*, by A. Grace Wenger and Dave and Neta Jackson. Instruct the leader to prepare a summary of the book and discussion questions for the group.

You will need

❑ two readers
❑ a storyteller
❑ flashlights
❑ an instrumentalist
❑ candles for "The Candlemakers' Contest": two tall candles, one taller than the other; two short candles in cup-like containers, one deeper than the other; trick birthday candles and a two little balls of modeling clay in which to stand them
❑ matches, a large glass jar, a Bible, pictures of Levi and Eli (hand drawn or magazine cut-outs) and tape
❑ slides, projector, and screen or video, television, and VCR
❑ speaker phone or letters from missionaries
❑ photo display of the missionaries your church supports
❑ a pop bottle band: flashlights, eight or more glass pop bottles, water, food coloring, players

---

Name of your church
Walking in the Light
Celebrating Missions

Gathering

Gathering Hymns ......"Be Thou my vision"
"When we walk with the Lord"

Words of Welcome

Call to Worship

Time with the Children ...."The Candlemaker's Contest"

Pop Bottle Band ...."This Little Light of Mine"

Scripture ....Isaiah 58:6-11

A Teaching: What Does It Mean to Walk in the Light?

Litany

Hymn of Response ...."Lord of light, your name outshining"

Letters from Missionaries

Hymn ....."Christian, let your burning light"

Offering ...."I bind my heart this tide" (quartet)

Working and Volunteering for Others

Hymn................"You are salt for the earth"

Benediction

Mission Centers
  1. Be Encouragers
  2. Learn About Local Missions
  3. Learn About Church Missions
  4. Discuss a Book on Missions
  5. Reenact "The Candlemaker's Contest"
  6. Make Candles
  7. Tell Stories of Mission
  8. Invite Friends to Church
  9. Walk in the "Light"

The Celebration

Gathering

Before the congregation arrives, darken the room and light a few candles on the worship table. Play upbeat recorded music as the congregation enters.

Gathering Hymns

Sing "Be thou my vision," "When we walk with the Lord," or other hymns that use images of discipleship or light.

Words of Welcome

Leader: Welcome to our Celebration of Missions Sunday, "Walking in the Light." During this service we will celebrate what it means to move from darkness into God's wonderful light and challenge everyone to reflect the light in everything we do and say.

Call to Worship

Two readers read these scriptures by flashlight to preserve the darkness of the room.

Reader One: This is the message we have heard from [Christ] and proclaim to you, that God is light and in him there is no darkness at all. If we say that we have fellowship with him while we are walking in darkness, we lie and do not do what is true; but if we walk in the light as he himself is in the light, we have fellowship with one another, and the blood of Jesus his Son cleanses us from all sin. (1 John 1:5-7)

Reader Two: Again Jesus spoke to the [people], saying, "I am the light of the world. Whoever follows me will never walk in darkness but will have the light of life." (John 8:12)

Time with the Children

Invite children to gather with the story-teller. As they are gathering, arrange props on a small table off to the side. Since the room is darkened, tell the story with the light of a flashlight or small lamp. Instruct the congregation to help tell the story by saying "OOOH," "AAAAAW" or "AAAAH" when cued. Tell "The Candlemaker's Contest" found in the resource section of this celebration.

Music

Pop bottle band plays "This Little Light of Mine."

Scripture

Isaiah 58:6-11
When the scripture reader reads the line "Then your light shall break forth like the dawn," slowly begin to bring the lights up in the room.

A Teaching: What Does It Mean to Walk in the Light?

The pastor or a lay person prepares a brief meditation based on the ideas and concepts presented in the introduction and Bible background for this celebration.

Litany

One: You are a chosen people, a royal priesthood, a holy nation, a people belonging to God, that you may declare the praises of him who called you out of darkness into his wonderful light. Once you were not a people, but now you are the people of God; once you had not received mercy, but now you have received mercy. (1 Peter 2:9 NIV)

Live as children of the light. (Eph 5:8b)

All: Loose the chains of injustice.
Untie the cords of the yoke.
Set the oppressed free.
Break every yoke.

Share your food with the hungry.
Provide the poor wanderer with shelter.
Clothe the naked.
Do not turn away your own flesh and blood.

One: Then your light will break forth like the dawn.
Your healing will quickly appear.
Then your light will rise in the darkness,
and your night will become like the noonday.

—based on Isaiah 58:6-8a,10b NIV

Hymn of Response

Sing "Lord of light, your name outshining" or other hymn using light imagery. Encourage the congregation to read silently through the words as a flute, violin, or cello plays an instrumental introduction.

Letters from Missionaries

Have readers of various ages and interests read the letters of encouragement from the missionaries to the congregation. Or hook up a speaker phone to call one of the missionaries your congregation supports. Let them give the congregation encouragement to be ambassadors for the gospel. Have the congregation sing the following hymn as a response to the missionaries while they are still on the line.

Hymn

"Christian, let your burning light"

Offering

A small ensemble sings "I bind my heart this tide" as an offertory (see Resources for This Celebration).

Working and Volunteering for Others

Show slides or a video of people in the congregation working or volunteering in service to others. Use musical accompaniment that is joyous. By now the room should be fully lighted.

Hymn

Sing "You are salt for the earth." Keep a lively tempo.

Benediction

One: We come to worship.

All: We go now to serve.

One: We have been given the light.

All: We go now to let it shine.

One: We have been blessed by God's love.

All: We go now to share it.

One: We are Christ's disciples.

All: We go now to witness to all.

By Jimmy Ross in *We Gather Together.*
Copyright © 1979 Brethren Press.

Mission Centers

Dismiss the congregation to go to Mission Centers.

1. Be Encouragers. Begin by making designs on cards, using torn pieces of construction paper. Write notes of encouragement to people who work in missions that your church supports. Use this time also to write notes of encouragement to others in the congregation.

2. Learn About Local Missions. Invite a representative of a local mission to give a presentation to the group. Ahead of time contact a person from a mission church nearby, a food pantry, a shelter, the Salvation Army, or a self-help handcraft shop.

3. Learn About Church Missions. Have your church's mission and service committee lead a session describing their goals, how they function, and their understanding of the needs of your church's community and your church's resources to meet those needs.

4. Discuss a Book on Missions. Discuss a book about mission, such as *Witness: Empowering the Church*, by A. Grace Wenger and Dave and Neta Jackson. Appoint someone to summarize the book or portions of it for the group and follow with a discussion.

5. Reenact "The Candlemaker's Contest." This center is particularly for the children to reenact and discuss the meaning of the story they heard in the celebration.

6. Make Candles. Do this activity in a kitchen. Collect a half-pint milk carton for each candle. Open the top of each carton completely. Help each candlemaker tie a wick to the middle of a pencil (wicks can be bought at craft stores, but a heavier cotton string will do). Place the pencil across the open carton so the wick hangs down in the middle of the carton. Carefully melt paraffin in several small sauce pans. Melt a different color of crayon with each pan of wax. Allow people to choose the color they would like to use. Pour a little wax in the bottom of a carton. Then have candlemakers drop in a couple of ice cubes. Pour in more wax. Add a few more ice cubes. Fill the remainder with wax. Allow the candle to harden for several hours. When the wax is solid, tear off the paper carton and snip off the pencil. You will have a short, square candle with unique holes in the sides.

7. Tell Stories of Mission. Invite one or several members of the congregation who have done or are doing voluntary service through a mission board, or otherwise, to share their stories of trials, victories, and lessons learned. Encourage youth to share their experiences, too. This is an opportunity to encourage young people to consider voluntary service in the future. Point out their gifts and issue them a call.

8. Invite Friends to Church. Ahead of time ask members of the congregation to donate old cards and magazines for this activity. To create an invitation, make new cards by cutting up the old cards and magazines. Have stamps and envelopes available, too, and offer to mail the cards right after the celebration.

9. Walk in the "Light." This activity physically illustrates how difficult it is to walk in darkness and how difficult it is to be a good guide. Divide the group into pairs and blindfold one of each pair. Then rearrange the room with chairs, tables, large blocks, or other obstacles. No speaking is allowed in the first variation of this blind walk. The blind partner places his or her hand on the shoulder of the guide. This hand/shoulder connection is the only way to communicate. The pair must walk around, through, and over the obstacles together. Try different speeds.

For another variation, rearrange the room. Blindfold the other partner and this time allow no touching. While the other pairs watch, one at a time, the guide talks the blind partner through the maze from one side of the room to the other. For a more complicated variation, have all of the blind partners traversing the room at the same time led by the voices of their guide partners who are on the opposite sides of the room, speaking at once. Finally, talk about the experience, expressing how it felt to be both guide and blind partner. What parallel does this allegory have for witnessing?

Resources for This Celebration

The Candlemaker's Contest

by Mariann Martin

Tape pictures of the candlemakers on the front of the table— Levi on the right and Eli on the left. This sets up the domain of the characters. Whenever one makes a candle, light the appropriate candle and place it on his side, above his picture.

Once upon a time, long, long ago, there lived two candlemakers who both made equally fine, beautiful candles that could light the soul as well as a room. Their names were Eli and Levi.

After graduating from candlemaking college, they both moved to a very dark village to set up shop. Eli chose a dark, narrow street where people would surely need candles. He put the beautiful candles in the windows, but he didn't light them. [*Put unlit candle above Eli's picture.*] Eli was afraid the people who had been in darkness so long might be blinded by the intrusion of light into their familiar dark world. "Besides," he thought, "everyone can tell this is a candle shop. I won't waste my profits. If people want to see how my candles work, they can come in and ask me and I'll be happy to light one for them." He sat down to wait for his customers.

After a few weeks, Eli despaired of how poorly the candle business was going. But as he sat glumly looking out of his shop window, he noticed a warm glow inside some of the houses on his dark street. The townspeople must be buying candles from someone else! He went for a walk to see what was going on. He turned the corner and there he saw it—Levi's shop! [*Place a candle above Levi's picture and light it.*] Eli noticed lighted candles in every window and a warm glow about the place. "All his profits are going up in smoke!" laughed Eli. "How can he afford to do that?" Then he noticed the customers buzzing in and out of the shop. "Wait a minute," thought Eli, "my candles are every bit as good as his! What's going on here?" He rolled up his sleeves and marched into the shop. "Listen, Levi, I was here first, how dare you . . . ," he began.

But just then a haggard little man stumbled into the shop. "Mr. Candlemaker," he said in a loud voice, "we need you!" Everyone stopped and stared at this strange little fellow. His hair was tousled, his clothes were askew, and he was covered with black and blue bruises! "I come from the Valley of the Harsh Winds," he said. "It is so dark there that we're always tripping and falling and hurting ourselves and each other. We need you to make a candle that can give us light in spite of the harsh winds," said the odd little man.

"Well, I'll do my best," said Levi.

"And I'll do even better!" shouted Eli, seeing a way to win some customers.

"Prove it!" said the little man. "Tomorrow both of you bring your best candles to the Valley of the Harsh Winds, and we'll buy from the one who makes the best candle."

All that night the candlemakers worked in their shops. The next day they packed up their candles and journeyed to the Valley of the Harsh Winds. All the people there were gathered in the darkness to see the light they so desperately needed.

Levi began with a tall candle with a long wick. [*Place tall candle on the right side and light it.*] "That should last a long time," he said as he lit it.

Eli smiled as he brought out an even taller candle with an even longer wick. [*Place a much taller candle on the left side and light it.*] "This will last much longer than that," he said. And there was light in the valley for the first time in a long time. All the people said, "OOOH, AAAAH!" [*Motion for the congregation and children to say oooh, aaaah.*]

But this was the Valley of the Harsh Winds. And when the winds saw the light, they gathered up, swooped down, and [*take a deep breath, motion children to do the same*] SWIIISH [*blow out the candles — the children will help*]. The winds blew out both candles. The people were so disappointed they all said, "AAAAAW." [*Ask the congregation to say it, too.*]

Undaunted, Levi brought out a short, plump candle cuddled in a cup. [*Place such a candle on the right side and light it.*] "This one should work on breezy nights," he said as he lit it.

"This one should stay lit and last a long time, too," said Eli as he lighted a fat candle with the wick deep down in the hollow of its own wax. [*Place such a candle on the left side and light it.*] And there was a beautiful light in the valley. The people all said, [*pause for congregation to get the cue*] "OOOH, AAAAH!"

But this was the Valley of the Harsh Winds. And when the winds saw the light, they joined together, swooped down, [*take a deep breath and indicate children do the same*] and SWIIISH! The wind blew out both fat candles. The people were so disappointed they said, "AAAAAW."

Now these were smart candlemakers. They were both well trained by the master candlemaker who always taught the principle of starting again. So they both brought out special candles that looked exactly alike. [*Bring out trick birthday candles set in balls of modeling clay or florist's clay.*] These candles looked a bit scrawny compared to the others, but the candlemakers smiled knowingly as they lit them.

Gracious me! Here we must stop to get a word from our sponsor—the master of candlemakers.

[*A person enters to read an advertisement. The storyteller looks in his or her direction. Reader speaks with a "commercial" voice.*] You are the light of the world. A city built on a hill cannot be hid. No one after lighting a lamp puts it under the bushel basket, but on the lampstand, and it gives light to all in the house. In the same way, let your light shine before others, so that they may see your good works and give glory to your Father in heaven. If you want to know more about the secrets of making light, the number to call is 1-800-Matthew 5:14-16! Now back to our story. [*Reader exits. Do not omit this part. The trick candles need to burn at least thirty seconds before they are blown out, or they won't relight.*]

[*Storyteller resumes.*] The candlemakers lit their tiny candles and the valley was filled with a beautiful light. All the people said, [*cue the congregation to say*] "OOOH, AAAAH!"

But this was the Valley of the Harsh Winds, and when the winds of darkness saw the light, they gathered up and swooped down [*cue children to blow*] and SWIIISH!! The winds blew out both scrawny candles. The people began to say, [*cue congregation*] "AAAAAW." But then a curious thing happened. These candles seemed to know about dealing with harsh winds. They lit right back up again. [*You may have to pause for the candles to relight or you may have to omit a sentence if they relight quickly. If they don't relight, simply use another match.*] And the people said, "OOOH, AAAAH!" But the winds gathered. [*take a deep breath*] SWIIISH! Darkness. The people disappointedly said "AAAAAW." But sure enough, the little candles came to life again.

And all the people said "Hurray!" and began to get out their checkbooks.

But Eli was a little nervous. How long would his candle hold up? He decided to make his candle completely windproof; then he would surely be the only winner of the contest. "Here is my very own special design," he announced. "I call it the NO CONTACT CANDLE!" [*Place a large clear jar upside down over the candle on the left. Press your hand on the top of it as you talk to be sure no air gets in under the rim.*]

Sure enough, this time when the winds gathered [*take a deep breath*] SWIIISH! Eli's candle didn't even feel it and Levi's candle blew right out! All the people shouted, "Hurray!" and began to write out their checks to Eli. But as they wrote, the light became dimmer and dimmer. The candle was so protected that it never felt the harsh winds, but neither did it have air to breathe. It slowly died out, never to relight again. [*Again adjust the sentences to end when the candle suffocates. If it is out and has been for a few seconds, you can lift the jar to dramatically unveil the dead candle. Smoke collected in the jar makes this a fun effect.*]

Levi's candle, though, revitalized by the fresh air, had flamed back to life once again.

And so all the people of the Valley of the Harsh Winds wrote out their checks to Levi instead. For he was a candlemaker who was not afraid to let his light shine!

The End.

Note: *Relight all the candles and allow them to burn at the front of the sanctuary.*

I bind my heart this tide

UNION 67. 77

1 I bind my heart this tide   to the Gal - i - le - an's side,   to the
2 I bind my soul this day   to the neigh - bor far a - way,   and the
3 I bind my heart in thrall   to the God, the Lord of all,   to the
4 I bind my - self to peace,   to make strife and en - vy cease. God,

wounds of Cal - va - ry,   to the Christ who died for   me.
stran - ger near at hand,   in this town, and in this land.
God, the poor one's friend,   and the Christ whom he did send.
knit thou sure the cord   of my thrall - dom to my Lord!   A - men.

Text: Lauchlan M. Watt, *The Tryst, A Book of the Soul*, 1907, alt.
Music: J. Randall Zercher, 1965, *The Mennonite Hymnal*, 1969

Resources

A World At Prayer: The New Exumenical Prayer Cycle. Mystic, Conn.: Twenty-Third Publications, 1990.

Appleton, George. *Jerusalem Prayers for the World Today.* London, England: Society for Promoting Christian Knowledge, 1989.

Aschliman, Kathryn, Ed. *Growing Toward Peace.* Scottsdale, Pa.: Herald Press, 1993.

Banquet of Praise: A Book of Worship Resources. Washington, D.C.: Bread for the World, 1990.

Bhagat, Shantilal. *God's Earth Our Home: A Resource for Congregational Study and Action on Environmental and Economic Justice.* National Council of Churches of Christ in the U.S.A., 1994.

Burstein, Chaya M. *The Jewish Kids Catalog.* Philadelphia, Pa.: The Jewish Publication Society of America, 1983.

Costello, Elaine, illus. *Religious Signing.* Toronto, Ont.: Bantam Books, 1986.

DeSola, Carla. *The Spirit Moves: A Handbook of Dance and Prayer.* Austin, Tex.: The Sharing Company, 1986.

Earth Stewardship Packet. Mennonite Central Committee. Akron, Pa.: MCC U.S. Global Education Office. Fall 1990.

Festival: Worship with Jesus, Worship Today. Nashville, Tenn.: Cokesbury, 1992.

Fifty Simple Things You Can Do to Save the Earth. Earth Works Group. Berkeley, Calif.: Earthworks Press, 1989.

Fry-Miller, Kathleen; Judith Myers-Walls; Janet Domer-Shank. *Peace Works.* Elgin, Ill.: Brethren Press, 1988.

Gerber, Suella; Kathleen Jansen; and Rosemary Widner. *Becoming God's Peacemakers.* Newton, Kan.: Faith and Life Press, 1992.

Books

Grishaver, Joel Lurie. *Building Jewish Life: Sukkot & Simhat Torah*. Los Angeles, Calif.: Torah Aura Productions, 1987.

In Spirit and in Truth: A Worship Book. Geneva, Switzerland: WCC Publications, 1991.

Luvmour, Sambhova and Jasette. *Everyone Wins! Cooperative Games and Activities*. Philadelphia, Pa.: New Society Publishers, 1990.

MacKenthun, Carole, and Paulinus Dwyer. *Peace*, Carthage, Ill.: Shining Star Publications, 1986.

Schlabach, Joetta Handrich. *Extending the Table: A World Community Cookbook*. Scottsdale, Pa.: Herald Press, 1991.

Weaver, Judy. *Celebrating Holidays and Holy Days in Church and Family Settings*. Nashville, Tenn.: Discipleship Resources, 1989.

With All God's People: The New Ecumenical Prayer Cycle. Geneva, Switzerland: WCC Publications, 1989.

Zimmerman, Martha. *Celebrate the Feasts*. Minneapolis, Minn.: Bethany House, 1981.

Music

Hymnal: A Worship Book
Brethren Press
1451 Dundee Avenue
Elgin, IL 60120
800 441-3712
or
Faith & Life Press
Box 347
Newton, KS 67114-0347
800 743-2484
or
Mennonite Publishing House
616 Walnut Avenue
Scottsdale, Pa 15683-1999
800 245-7894

Jewish Liturgical Music
Purple Pomegranate Productions
80 Page Street
San Francisco, CA 94102

Teaching Peace (audiocassette) by Red Grammar
The Children's Bookstore Distribution
67 Wall Street, Suite 2411
New York, NY 10005

EcuFilm (an ecumenical film/video distribution service)
810 Twelfth Avenue South
Nashville, TN 37203
800 251-4091

Shalom Lifestyles (youth video curriculum)
Mennonite Media Productions
1251 Virginia Ave.
Harrisburg, VA 22801-2497
800 999-3534

sources